W9-BAP-118

MERLIN

The Sorcerer's
GUIDE
TO SURVIVAL
in College

Christopher F. Monte

Manhattanville College

☆ Wadsworth Publishing Company ☆
Belmont, California ☆ A Division of Wadsworth, Inc.

English Editor: Angela M. Gantner
Production Editor: Leland Moss
Interior Design: Andrew H. Ogus
Cover Design: Nancy Brescia
Illustrator: Steve Kongsle
Print Buyer: Barbara Britton
Compositor: Janet Tumpich
Copy Editor: Anne Montague
Editorial Assistant: Julie Johnson
Signing Representative: Ira Zukerman
Consulting Editor: Henry Staat

© 1990 by Christopher F. Monte. All rights reserved. No part of this book may be reproduced, stored in a retrieval system, or transcribed, in any form or by any means, electronic, mechanical, photocopying, recording, or otherwise, without the prior written permission of the publisher, Wadsworth Publishing Company, Belmont, California 94002, a division of Wadsworth, Inc.

Printed in the United States of America   49

    2   3   4   5   6   7   8   9   10—94   93   92   91   90

Library of Congress Cataloging-in-Publication Data
Monte, Christopher F.
    Merlin : the sorcerer's guide to survival in college / Christopher
F. Monte.
        p.   cm.
    Includes bibliographical references.
    ISBN 0-534-13482-3
    1. College student orientation – United States.   I. Title.
LB2343.32.M66   1990
378.1 '98–dc20   89-48599
                                                          CIP

 M

For C. J. and T. K.

The sorcery is yours.

Love,

Uncle Merlin

 **M**

Merlin Words:

☆ Studenting (noun): the art of compre-
hending words and pictures and skill in
using them to communicate ideas

☆ To student (verb): anticipating the consequences of one's own behavior and the
behavior of one's teachers to facilitate
studenting

☆ Sorcerer: one who casts lots, reads the
signs, and predicts

Contents

CONTENTS

CONTENTS

Contents

About Merlin

Merlin knew the secret of the Universe: Knowledge is words and pictures. If you treasure words and pictures, learn to manipulate them, to rely on them, to sequence them so they are meaningful to others, you have more power than all the sorcerers through history. You are an educated person.

This survival guide has no magic formulae. What knowledge it contains is based on contemporary and classical psychological research and theory. It is seasoned with practical experiences drawn from 20 years of teaching, and almost twice that number studenting.

Survival sorcery in college is a learnable set of skills for dealing with words, pictures, and the people who will try to share their favorite words and pictures with you. You have to learn the art of mastering the languages of words and pictures while ignoring how intimidated you feel, how bored you may become, or how tired you grow. *Merlin* skills are for 18-year-old first-year students and for 55-year-old first-year returning students.

Many things can be learned from *Merlin*. You will not like some of them. Others you will find irrelevant. And still others will strike you as absolutely wrong. You're free, of course, to dismiss the ideas, argue with them, or make use of them. I present a particularly narrow minded viewpoint here, one that is biased toward my conception of "excellence." I'm pretty sure the psychological sorcery I offer is sound

even when it appears strange. But if you disagree with the ideas in
Merlin, don't change them, don't try to improve them. Write your own
survival guide and ignore mine, thank you.

One of the things you ought to be learning in college is how to
judge the quality of information. When you've finished this guide,
you're free to judge it deficient or wrong or irrelevant. I hope your
judgment will be different from any of these. But first you have to read
Merlin. Please accept my invitation, for I think that we will both profit. I
would be grateful for your ideas, suggestions, and disagreements (also
any kind words you might have handy). As time passes, and my
experience grows, I will probably change some parts of *Merlin*. Perhaps with your help, the changes can be richer and more valuable. The
last page of *Merlin* provides a tear-out sheet that can be used to give
the author some feedback. You can contact me at Manhattanville
College, 125 Purchase Street, Purchase, New York 10577.

If you are or plan to be a psychology major, you will find many of
the examples congenial and familiar. And if you are a major in another
discipline who is interested in making your college years productive
and memorable, you will find most of the content applicable to your
pursuit of a liberal arts education. Virtually all *Merlin* techniques are
very adaptable by anyone who cares to try.

Theoretical and Practical *Merlin*

It might be of some help to understand that this survival guide is
divided between very practical, "how to do it" advice and some more
abstract kinds of knowledge that make the practical advice sensible.
Theoretical Merlin is usually found at the beginnings of chapters. Large
parts of each chapter are *Practical Merlin* guides on how to do something. As you might expect most chapters are mixtures of both kinds of
ideas. Chapter One, however, is completely a *Theoretical Merlin*
enterprise. The central theme embodied throughout the various parts
of *Merlin* is the notion that accurate anticipation is realistic control.
Knowing what to expect enhances your capacity to cope. *Merlin*
sorcery is nothing more or less than anticipation.

What Merlin Cannot Do for You

There are a variety of self-help and "sucess in college" books available. My understanding of the ones I've seen is that they aim to help students get their diplomas. Such books focus on "success" in college, with an implied definition of success as getting to graduation in one piece.

Merlin aims at a different target. The goal in these pages is to help you participate in your education, with the natural consequence of obtaining a diploma that reflects the educational level you achieved.

Put bluntly: *Merlin*, unlike other "how to succeed" books, does not attempt to make college easier, does not give you "tricks" to get by without substantive effort, and cannot teach you rote routines to "play student" in order to survive sufficiently well to graduate. Rather than "how to get to graduation," *Merlin* is a "how to proceed with your learning on the way to graduation" survival manual.

Instead of getting your diploma without necessarily getting an education, *Merlin* can teach you to "get" an education on the way to the diploma.

I doubt whether a student who is as yet ill prepared to cope with the rigors of college at least at the average level will find coping with this guide possible or desirable. *Merlin will enhance your own natural strengths; it will not create them without raw materials.* My belief is that any student with a strong enough wish to survive and to prosper will find the sorcerery in this manual useful and understandable in the same way that a "Dutch Uncle's" often painful advice is useful and understandable.

Merlin can teach you:
- How your personality regulates your performance
- Proper care and feeding of professors
- To treasure the power of words and pictures
- How to get teachers to teach you
- How to get advisors to advise you
- How to study a textbook
- How to take tests
- How to choose a major
- Survival with your sanity intact
- Some ugly truths that will grow more beautiful

Who Was That Masked Sorcerer?

There are a number of historical, and probably apocrophyl, accounts of the magician Merlin. In this survival guide, I can only recount what I know to be gospel truth from my first hand experiences with my uncle Merlin. It may dispel some myths to know that uncle Merlin was at the court of King Arthur and served for many years as the King's personal sorcerer and manicurist. It was Arthur, in fact, who bestowed an affectionate nickname on uncle Merlin after a particularly irksome morning spent trying to introduce the King to a relatively new culinary delight, the bagel. King Arthur's delighted exclamation when he understood that a bagel is not a doughnut was: "Merlin—you are a wiley knave with true magic!" From that day, Merlin was known as "wiley," which eventually corrupted to "Willy." To avoid being referred to as "Willy," uncle Merlin temporarily changed his name to Murray. And he left King Arthur's court to reappear in history in London during the reign of Queen Victoria. During his London incarnation, Uncle Merlin adopted the name Mycroft Holmes, and was known to historians as the indolent but smarter brother of the esteemed Sherlock Holmes. How uncle Merlin made his way into contemporary academia is a bit of a family puzzle. Nevertheless it is with gratitude and family pride that we profit here, then, from the wisdom of Murry Mycroft Merlin, my uncle the sorcerer.

Welcome to *Merlin.*

MERLIN

Merlin had a pointy hat.
But he took it off in elevators.

About This Chapter

Main Theme of the Chapter

Students survive in college in ways that range from emotionally draining to admirably productive. Each form of survival stems from the student's personality style:

☆ *Darwin* students, who defy teachers to teach

☆ *Damocles* students, who are too frightened to learn

☆ *Merlin* students, who anticipate realistically and control gently but powerfully from this capacity to anticipate what happens next

Related Ideas

Simple but unpleasant truths about:

☆ Enduring frustration, boredom, and anxiety

☆ How important grades really are

☆ Establishing a workable academic reputation

☆ Being self-reliant

CHAPTER 1

Student Survival Styles

To be in college is to be for a time in an alien world. Someone has suddenly changed the rules for your life. You recall wanting this adventure for yourself, but because there is so much anxiety and newness, you can no longer remember why.

There are pressures. Demands made by professors. School requirements for everything from where you will park your car to when you will eat your meals to what courses you have to have.

Pressures. Parents have expectations. They voice some of them. But they only imply others. If you are the first or one of the first people in your family to attend college, the pressures are tripled. Your parents' and grandparents' wishes for you are strong. They will be happy if you succeed. They will be proud if you become a college graduate. Do they really know what you have to go through?

More pressures. You get an adviser. He or she tells you that you will make several important, life-changing decisions in the near future. You should decide on a major, decide whether to go on to professional study in graduate school, law school, medical school, veterinary school, decide on a minor or second area of concentration, decide between two sections of the same required course. . . . Decide!

Internal pressures. You know in your heart that you don't know who you are. Yet. Secretly, you're convinced that you're really not as smart as you pretend to be. Nor are you as strong, or as clever, or as sure of your own success as you portray publicly. Deep in the place where you talk only to yourself, you're certain that you know less than you pretend to know. That's why you're here, you tell yourself. "I will learn to decode the mysteries that others seem to have solved."

You know, too, in that same special, private place that you want some time to play with life. You're not completely ready to devote your whole being to the scholarly life. "Scholarly life? I don't even know who the hell I am! And I'm scared."

A person may survive these pressures—even, perhaps, master the uncertainties. The question is not whether you will survive, but how?

Three Survival Styles

The first lesson *Merlin* can teach you is that you *will* survive. You can take some comfort in the knowledge that every student is apprehensive about his or her success and equally uncertain as you are about personal competence. They will survive. And you will survive. But none of you knows that at the outset. You will even graduate with a diploma. Very probably.

The quality of that survival and the substance behind that diploma, however, are under your control. Styles of survival, each associated with some unpleasant truths, have to be faced and then embraced or rejected. Here are the three styles I have observed over and over through twenty years of teaching. Each style works, but each has a very different price tag. I've named the styles after prominent intellectual figures in somewhat whimsical fashion. But if you know the historical figure for whom a style is named, you'll detect the whimsy—and the accuracy.

Darwinian Survival

Darwin students are angry. They are angry with their parents, with their peers, with their teachers, with the world. Every action is a struggle. Every situation is a competition for power or possession. They compete against the demands of the college, against their peers, against themselves.

Darwins are continually hungry for someone to give them what they want. And what they want, they want *now*, be it a girl- or boyfriend to date, a car to drive, a sweater to wear, or a college degree to display. God help those who get in the way when a Darwin sets his or her sights on something.

Students who enter college without a clear idea of the difference between what they want and what they can reasonably ask for from the institution are doomed to a Darwinian existence.

Darwin students do not trust anything that comes without a fight. If there is no reason to fight, they become bored, apathetic, detached. When there is a reason to fight, they are formidable. Not successful, or productive—just formidable. As Charles Darwin, the creator of the first scientifically acceptable theory of evolution, pointed out in 1859, animals enjoy survival success by adapting to the environment they occupy. Darwin students act as though the college campus is a primeval battleground where their success depends on everyone else's failure. The hunger that impels them can be satisfied only by themselves. But they don't know that. And most Darwins never will.

Advisers and professors soon learn that it is not possible to "feed" or to nourish a Darwin survivor. Such students won't permit nourishment. Reason, persuasion, and brute intimidation are usually attempted by some teacher or dean at one or another moment in the Darwin's college career. None of these crude efforts will succeed. They merely provoke a higher level of combativeness from the Darwin and such a degree of perverse enjoyment that the struggle for survival is perpetuated rather than diminished.

CHAPTER ONE

The "cure" for the Darwin is the realization, however attained (and it is a mystery to me how some Darwins finally learn this), that knowledge is not a possession one has to compete for before it's all gone. A college diploma is not a badge that certifies the intellectual superiority of those who "own" one. The college campus is not an arena in which to dare professors to teach you something useful. Most professors loathe dares. But their hearts melt at the sound of an earnest question.

A college education is a process. It is not a thing. It is not a commodity. The process happens inside people, and it changes how much of the world they will see and what they will do about it. Even if you wanted to get a college education, there is no *thing* to get. You get a diploma at graduation, but in fact it is more correct to say that you

M

Dear Darwin:

Your strength lies not in your desire to battle the system, but in your passion to defeat your own ignorance.

Dreamfully yours,

Merlin

earned a degree of education or knowledge or skill that is represented by the diploma. The diploma merely reflects substantial intellectual changes in the person who earned it.

Damocles Survival

A more nerve-racking way to survive college is practiced by those who believe they are in a hostile environment where disaster will strike at any second. Disaster may take different forms; even the most mundane daily activity requires a fresh act of courage from the Damocles student. To be a Damocles is to be exhausted.

Every test, every paper, every assignment, every interaction with a professor or peer is fraught with fear. The Damocles student feels like the historical character in Ancient Greece of the same name waiting endlessly for the sword to drop from its thread onto his head. And Damocles was just eating dinner at the time! The student is trapped by the demands of college and can respond only with ever-increasing anxiety and distress.

The Damocles student has what psychologist J. W. Atkinson calls a "fear of failure" personality style. Intense fear of failure can pervade a student's whole existence. It generalizes from classroom situations to any situation where one's competence may be tested publicly.

Fear-of-failure people operate unrealistically. Sometimes Damocles students choose very simple, unchallenging tasks or courses because these pose little threat of failure. Note that such easy tasks also provide very little real satisfaction or merit even when one succeeds. But Damocles students sometimes choose goals that are difficult (sometimes even impossible) to attain, because failing to reach a really difficult goal carries no shame. A more realistic goal poses a *real* test of one's competence and is therefore most threatening. Damocles students tackle courses and attempt to prepare for careers way out of line with their actual abilities. For example, one student I knew could not get beyond basic math courses, failed virtually every science

M

Dear Damocles:

Your strength lies not in your ability to predict failure, but in your ability to predict.

Oracularly yours,

Merlin

course she attempted, and was, when I met her, trying to take an advanced physics course. The chairman of the physics department, naturally, was reluctant to accept her. He was amazed when she told him she needed the course to get into medical school!

This Damocles clearly had little insight into the unrealistic quality of her goals, and how disproportionate these goals were to her own past achievements. But by pursuing the impossible, she was far less anxious, far less guilty for failures, and far less shamed than she would be had she pursued more realistic paths.

The problem for this Damocles was that her strategy did not work for long. Eventually, this kind of unrealistic risk taking no longer succeeds in avoiding the pain of real tests of personal competence.

Failure avoidance at this level accomplishes one thing: total failure. The Damocles becomes emotionally and physically spent. College life is a continuing nightmare. Failure avoidance results in complete lack of success.

Damocles survival behavior has a hidden benefit. If one plays at Damocles long enough, one becomes a pitiful victim. Such blatant psychological distress as that exhibited by the confirmed Damocles encourages other students, faculty, and parents to rescue the over-whelmed victim.

I have known deans who have bent college regulations to rescue a Damocles where they would have permitted a Darwin to sink. I know parents who wrote papers for their Damocles offspring, and teachers who spent hours helping a Damocles pass an examination largely by continuous trial and guess. (The student passed the course with a D, and the institution, the student, and the subject matter were all impoverished in this episode.) Who was the real victim in each of these rescues?

Merlin Survival

Merlin is sorcery. The Merlin strategy, therefore, is a magic strategy of survival. But *magic* is used in this guide as being synonymous with *know-how*. The particular brand of know-how is psychology.

The Merlin student is not any brighter or any more knowledgeable than Darwin or Damocles peers. Anxiety is no stranger to a Merlin. Confusion about personal identity is as intense in a Merlin as in a Darwin or a Damocles. And a Merlin has no fewer fantasies of success, power, and unlimited happiness than non-Merlins.

But the Merlins I have come to know are different from Darwins and Damocleses. The crucial difference is threefold: Two parts are as pragmatic and as concrete as a button and its hole, and one part is nearly ineffable. Yet when you see it, you'll recognize it.

The first concrete quality of Merlins that distinguishes them from non–Merlin peers is a history of exposure to the written word. Books, magazines, diary keeping as a hobby, interactive and verbal computer games were all part of Merlins' growing-up. Almost always they take the written word for granted in the sense that words are friends, sources of information and enjoyment. And the Merlins I have known adopted this view by watching the important people in their lives. Uncle Merlin wants me to point out that love of words and facility with them are not qualities wired into a person's brain. If your previous exposure to or interest in reading and writing is not extensive, such privations are not irrevocable. In fact, college is one of the best times in your life to cultivate a love of words and pictures.

The second concrete quality of Merlin survivors is their skill at finding out things they don't know—the skill of acquiring new skills. They never hesitate to ask, to look, to browse, to experiment, to try, to tinker with, to borrow, to beg, to imitate. Merlins look around and adopt from others what they observe. They try out roles, unafraid to momentarily be something other than what they have been. Merlins learn from professors and peers by paying attention to the important signals these people send.

It's not genetic, by the way. It is a learnable skill. More important, Merlins imitate models of learning and problem solving because they get satisfaction from it. In their lives, imitation of resourceful learners was somehow rewarded.

The last quality, and one that is difficult if not impossible to express directly, is the Merlin's true magic. Here are some feeble attempts to describe it:

- Merlins are *psychologically minded:* They monitor self and reflect on feelings and thoughts before acting.

- Merlins delight in all forms of expression, from writing to drawing to dancing to sculpting, but they feel *no need to advertise their delight or their expertise ostentatiously,*

- Merlins have restrained *gentleness* coupled with a wry or off-center sense of humor. They sense and appreciate the absurd.

Such humor punctures pretensions without wounding. (You'll know it when you see it.) Put crudely: Merlins cherish words and pictures, can put themselves in the place of another, learn from and imitate accomplished learners, and they are gentle, even in humor. Their humor is frequently an antidote for pretentiousness.

I do not know if the gentleness is an essential quality. I do know that it is an appealing one that draws other people to Merlins and enriches everyone the Merlin interacts with.

The Hard Part: Four Merlin Truths

At the turn of the century, Sigmund Freud told us in a compelling way what philosophers had been telling us for centuries: We are quite capable of lying to ourselves. Self-deception is usually a psychological defense we use to protect ourselves from a piece of reality we find threatening. It is typical for the "threat" to be some perceived danger to our cherished conception of ourselves.

Merlins lie to themselves less frequently than Darwins or Damocleses. They permit themselves to see through their own pretenses most of the time. Not always, mind you. In the present context, there are four rather unpleasant truths about college work that have to be faced. They concern three of our most cherished self-deceptions: pleasure-pain, impressing others, and grades.

We lie to ourselves about these issues; college catalogs perpetuate the lies, and admissions offices frequently do nothing to correct them. Once in college, students are surprised that some commonly accepted truisms evaporate under the pressure of college demands. Here are the unpleasant Merlin truths.

Professor to Merlin: Marx has said that "Religion is the opiate of the masses."
Merlin to Professor: Groucho?

1. If It Hurts, You're Doing It Right!

The self-deception involved here is the widely held belief that the college or university is responsible for "giving" a student an "education." (Or it is sometimes phrased this way: The college has to guarantee that a student will be educated at the time of graduation.) If a student remains an ignoramus after four years of "study" at Boing College, then Boing College is said to have "failed" the student.

It is true, certainly, that colleges and universities exist in widely varying degrees of quality. Some colleges are truly junk food for the mind. But properly credentialed institutions with legitimate faculties offer the *possibility* of an education, the *opportunity* to study, the *occasion* to work with accomplished thinkers. It is the student who must avail himself or herself of these resources.

The university or college educates no one. Each student exerts effort and persistence to learn. It is a first-person, active process, not a third-person, passive one. It is the student's sweat and tears that accomplish this worthwhile process called "getting an education." Whom do we congratulate at graduation—the student or the faculty?

If the university educated people, then the school should receive the diploma. The president should get the graduation presents. And the faculty should congratulate itself, whereas the student and his/her family should be as blase as if the new graduate had simply bought a new suit.

☆ ★ ☆

Parents to graduate: So they finally made you a college
    graduate?
Graduate: Yeah, and for another $75,000, they'll make
    me a lawyer.
Parents: So how much for a brain surgeon?

Students sometimes complain that some courses are hard, or some professors demand too much, or some readings are "impossible." One of my students even said that a book I assigned "hurt her head." Another of my students, a Merlin if ever there was one, mustered all the grace at her command and said: "If it hurts, you're doing it right."

Most of your efforts in college will, and should, cost you something in personal pleasure and comfort. There are moments of fun in college. But the business of college, the actual learning, costs effort, and time, and frustration tolerance. Ideas are not cheap. As the athletes say, "No pain, no gain."

Recognizing this simple, unpleasant truth automatically gives you more than 50 percent of the resources you will need to persist and to make a success of college life.

2. Substance Before Style. Always.

A number of phrases capture the essence of this self-deception. "It's not what you know, but who you know that counts." "The old-boy network." The insidious aspect of these expressions is that they are true in part. That is to say, they work some of the time.

What makes them self-deceiving strategies is that they do not work over the long haul. In fact, a college career, which typically consists of four or more years of work, could not be sustained by a person who operates only out of appealing style and charm.

At the most primitive level, some students believe that a well-worded but shallow essay answer or a stylishly prepared folder to hold an empty term paper will somehow magically result in a better grade. If a professor actually reads the work, its folder or elaborate wording will belie the student's lack of substance.

At a slightly more sophisticated social level, some students believe personal sociability that impresses others favorably will earn high grades and academic success. The simple truth is that in college the quality of your thinking—judged largely through what you write—will earn more respect and higher grades than wearing the "right" clothes or associating with the "right" people. If you don't know your stuff, your teachers' opinions of you and your grades will reflect your ignorance.

CHAPTER ONE

You can learn your stuff only if you study. Sometimes, despite what you may have heard, that means *memorizing* notes or textbook concepts. You can't run a furnace without fuel. Memorized facts and ideas are fuel. Later on, those memories will help you to do other things, such as abstract the concepts, generalize them to new situations, or even create a unique synthesis of familiar ideas. But no student can do this without first getting the concepts and facts into his or her brain.

Memorizing gets a lot of bad press. Nevertheless, it is an important skill. You will not pass biology, psychology, and many history, language, accounting, and philosophy courses without memorizing ideas and whole lists of facts. Sounds awful, doesn't it?

People generally argue that memorizing ideas and facts leads to "parroting" ideas rather than truly "learning" them. Nothing could be further from the truth. First, get facile enough with an idea to parrot it verbatim. Then, even without deliberate awareness, the stored information will begin to undergo transformations. You will build on ideas to acquire new ones, extend them to problems you would not have even recognized, and begin to have your own ideas about many of the facts and concepts to which you exposed your grateful brain.

Memorizing is not equivalent to parroting. Without memorizing, it is unlikely that you will store enough information as you study the elementary portions of many disciplines to permit you to advance much beyond the level of "I think I heard that idea before."

It is much more like buying a road map to enable you to see places others can help you visit. A lot of what you memorize you will gradually forget. But you will have a sense of familiarity with the material that will smooth relearning it, or pave the way to learning related ideas. The improved facility in relearning is what pioneering psychologists called "savings." In fact, the rate of speed for *reacquiring* previously learned information is a sensitive measure of how much the learner has actually changed from the initial experience of learning.

Please note, however, that there is a substantial difference between the glib student who attempts to wing it through verbal facility with memorized facts and ideas and the serious student who has struggled to acquire a working vocabulary and understanding of the basics. Substance before style, and then real style with precision is possible.

☆ ★ ☆

Psychology prof lecturing to class: Modern cognitive
psychology has shown that much of human forgetting is
really a failure to retrieve stored information rather
than loss of the information completely.
Student: Could you repeat that?

☆ ★ ☆

3. Grades Aren't Essential. They're Everything!

Grades have different meanings to different people. There was a time
in our academic history when we tried to minimize grading or convince ourselves that it didn't matter. We even went so far as to substitute lengthy written evaluations for numerical and letter grades on a
student's transcript. No one was happy with these "improvements"
for long.

One motive that governed these simpleminded remedies to the distress caused by grading was the belief that grades are basically unfair
and subjective indicators of a student's worth. Part of this belief is
accurate. No grade is a reflection of a student's worth. *Ever.*

On the whole, though, grades do reflect fairly a student's level of
achievement relative to others in the same class. No matter what the
grade—good, poor, or mediocre—it tells nothing about that student's
worth, humanity, or goodness. But grades say a lot about the student's level of academic achievement, effort, and performance. To
believe anything else is a monumental self-deception.

Most teachers, but certainly not all of them, work hard to grade
accurately in terms of what they have assigned and what their experience shows students at a given level are able to do. There are usually
differences in how teachers assign A's and B+'s, and more differences
in how A's and A–'s are assigned.

But in my experience, there are few differences in how experienced
teachers view C's and D's and F's. A student who earns *generally* a C
or C+ average would not suddenly become an A or B+ student with
different teachers. The move from a C level to a B+ or A– level can
occur only when the overall quality of the student's work has changed
substantially.

CHAPTER ONE

To say the same thing another way, teachers, despite their human foibles and biases, *generally* do not assign grades capriciously. It is not a game, not a strategy of power plays or even of petty revenges. After two or four or six semesters of earning a general overall C or C+ index in all the courses taken, you can be pretty sure that the student is working at the C level. It's no accident. And I am almost certain it's not unfair.

The second self-deception about grades that we like to entertain to protect self-esteem is the belief that "grades are not really the important thing about a college education." True, the grade is not important any more than the thermometer that records your fever is important. Both assessment devices are only reflections of the process they attempt to monitor.

But a kind of reverse snobbery that borders on foolhardiness is represented in the belief that grades are merely the "elitist requirements of the establishment." The only thing I can see that qualifies as "elite" about grades assigned by experienced teachers is that they separate poor students from mediocre ones from very good ones.

Whoever told you that grades are not the important thing was wrong. Every person intuitively knows that getting an A or B+ is better than getting a C+ or D. We may not all be able to achieve A's and B's, but the way the world works, higher grades mean higher levels of effort, higher achievements attained, and higher expectations for the future performance of the person who earned the higher grades.

ELLSWORTH FREUD, BROTHER OF SIGMUND, BUT KNOWN BEST FOR HIS DISCOVERY OF THE PHENOMENON OF UNDERWEAR ENVY.

When major corporations recruit, when graduate schools and professional schools screen candidates for admission, and when potential employers who require a college diploma interview prospective trainees, you'd better believe they review a person's grades. And you had better know in your heart that *they* take grades seriously.

STUDENT SURVIVAL STYLES

A few years ago, when colleges were in uproar over demands from student activists to change the system, grading, for a time, ceased being a relatively accurate reflection of a student's academic competence. Employers, graduate and professional schools, and government agencies soon learned not to trust the mere possession of a college diploma or the transcript of a B average as being a reliable indicator of college-level skills and intelligence.

For a time, these institutions had to rely on their own assessment techniques to insure that so-called college graduates with a *record* of achievement in art, science, language, mathematics, psychology, and so on actually had the cognitive and motivational competencies the records indicated. Bitter complaints from all kinds of social critics followed.

The focus of the complaints was the so-called inflation of the grading systems and the corruption of the value of a college education. Colleges across the United States took the complaints seriously, and for now it is unlikely that professors will treat their grades as "elitist necessities" to be hurriedly assigned and dismissed. And neither should you.

Be aware that professors take grades seriously, that the college takes them seriously, that professional and graduate schools take them seriously—and all of us put our faith in the honesty and relative accuracy of grades. Grades are the only comparative measure we have, and we behave as if we believe in them.

So grades count. Earning as high a grade as you can in a course is the reason you attended college. Not, I hasten to add, to obtain the *grade*. But to obtain the grade as a reflection of what you learned. It is a simple-minded, brutal, unpleasant truth. But it is a Merlin truth.

The hidden premise in this argument that makes it acceptable to me is that grades are an accurate (most of the time) reflection of a student's attainments. If not for that link, I would find grades an annoyance. You may disagree. Please remember I am speaking of a student's *average* grades across many courses, not of *one* poor or even of *one* excellent grade. Safety (and accuracy) lies in numbers. The Merlin student knows these things intuitively and practices these rituals obsessively:

• Expect hard work that sometimes tires and sometimes exhausts you.

• Rarely, preferably never, attempt to wing it when you really haven't studied or prepared. Always study, always prepare, unless you're having open heart surgery. In that case, have your roommate bring your books to the hospital so you can study before and after the operation.

- Work like hell at full tilt all the time to achieve the highest grades possible. You will surprise yourself and find you have achieved the highest level of intellectual growth as well.

4. Self-Reliance Is Reliable. And Required.

Individualized education at a small college has its academic and emotional advantages when compared to the feeling of being lost in the teeming crowd of a large university. In the smaller, largely private liberal arts institutions, the incoming student is less likely to feel intimidated by the novelty and demands of college. Some people argue that the small, usually liberal arts–oriented institution permits the student to make the transition to college life more easily and provides more attention to the individual's unique psychological and educational needs.

The reality is, of course, more complex. Some smaller institutions are indeed very adept by tradition and philosophy at enhancing the individual's intellectual and emotional growth. Certainly the sense of security can be greater than in a larger university. Students in the smaller schools may feel they are learning more from their personal contacts with professors and mentors than students who are packed into lecture halls with 300 of their peers.

But many of us do find our way into larger institutions where mass lectures are the order of the day, where being a freshman means that you are one of thousands of people on campus. You may take courses that have graduate student assistants teaching much of the material, and, as a friend of Merlin says, you'll have to bring binoculars just to see a professor. Even in the smaller institutions, however, students may very well discover professors who are as unreachable as those in the larger institutions. By the same token, many professors in the larger universities transcend the system and its numbers to provide as much individualized attention as in the small schools. And one could argue that the student experience at a large university has its own advantages in social, emotional, and intellectual variety.

STUDENT SURVIVAL STYLES

The point is that when you enter college, whether it is a large university or small school, you must be prepared to rely on yourself. The days of high school spoon-feeding are over. No one will monitor your daily activities. No one will tell you to get your reading done or to write your papers. No one will direct your library searches for information. No one will help you take notes in lectures or clue you in when it's time to prepare for exams. You will do these things. To a great degree, but not completely, you are on your own. And you are supposed to be. What should happen inside your brain during your college years can't happen unless you are in charge of it.

Part of the educational process is the increased independence that comes through learning to trust your own judgment and competence. It is a scary experience, especially when you are in a new environment with many demands.

The Merlin truth that you need to keep foremost in mind is this: No one ever died from self-reliance. Dependence on teachers or the institution is akin to vampirism: without self-direction, courage, and the preparedness that comes from anticipation, you will be a sucker in more ways than one. If sudden independence makes you anxious, then you are normal. If the anonymity of large classes intimidates you, then you are perceptive. If you feel frustrated by the trial and error needed to make things work, then you are intelligent. If you expect professors and advisers to attend to your needs, you're a sucker.

There is another side to this discussion: the question of motivation to be in college in the first place. Some students, newly graduated from high school, are simply not ready, both motivationally and intellectually, to attend college. They would profit from some time away from school because it is frequently true that the passage of time alone yields added maturity.

Merlin's father was adamant: "When you graduate high school," he told the young sorcerer, "you will go to college. Or you will be a wart on the rump of a swine. For eternity." Merlin, therefore, had clear family expectations and external motivation to attend college, even if he didn't have a clue about why he might want to be there.

CHAPTER ONE

Many students attend college because of the pressure of parental expectation. Others go because they frankly don't have anything else to do. Neither of these reasons is sound, because the demands made on the student directly test the student's capacities to tolerate frustration, delay immediate gratifications, and grow more intellectually flexible and self-reliant. If you detect in yourself a puzzling lack of direction, if you know that academics is simply not your cup of tea at this moment in your life, or if you sense that you are not a self-starter, it may be wise to delay the continuation of your college education.

Note, however, that *every* college freshman puzzles over issues of personal identity. Many are tentative about what career path they want to follow and what major might get them there. These uncertainties are normal and should not deter you from a college education. In fact, they are very good reasons to attend college. But at the more personal level, when you sense that your current personal style does not mesh with spending four or more years in an environment that expects self-reliance and persistence, then consider taking a leave of absence.

The more mature students who come to college after years of attending to their family or career are the exceptions who prove the rule. Experienced people such as these are hungry for an education. They are eager to advance themselves intellectually and emotionally, and although they may be anxious or intimidated by the prospect, they have the maturity and desire to meet the challenge with dignity. Older students may not know any more clearly exactly what they want from college, but they know they want college. And it is that hunger, born from experience without an education, that sustains them. They are Merlin's star students.

Some Summary, Some Conclusions

☆ College makes emotional and intellectual demands that will cost you much.

☆ Survival can be painful or profitable:

- Darwin: combative, egocentric, and never satisfied

- Damocles: fearful, passive, and victimlike

- Merlin: realistic, resourceful, questioning, and gentle

☆ The Merlin student knows:

- If it hurts, you're doing it right.

- Substance before style. Always.

- Grades count; work for good ones.

- Spoon-feeding is over. Rely on yourself.

☆

Merlin couldn't understand why his
symbol was a quarter moon.
He felt he was a full mooner, at least.

About This Chapter

Main Theme of the Chapter
Talking reveals you. When two people talk, both are exposed,
and the exposure results in some problematic interactions.
Talking to professors takes some Merlin skill, because
student personality style can clash dramatically with
professor personality style.

Related Ideas
Here are some ways to identify and to relate appropriately to
troublesome professors and still participate in your own education. You will learn the care and feeding of the:

☆ Arrogant prof

☆ Narcissistic prof

☆ Indifferent prof

☆ Obsessive prof

☆ Merlin prof

CHAPTER 2

The Care and Feeding of Professors

Talking is the most immediate behavioral product of our brains. When we speak, we want people to accept what we say as meaning our meanings. But, as we have all experienced, our meanings are not always received by others in the form we intended.

Sometimes people detect unintended meanings embedded in what we say. If they are sophisticated listeners, they will respond more strongly to a hidden meaning than to the surface one. When there is a conflict between what we mean to say and what our listeners hear us saying, we need a way to clarify our statements and increase their precision and reliability. Or we must suffer the consequences of having people wonder whether we mean what we say.

For short periods in your life, imprecise speech is not particularly troublesome. In general, the discrepancy between what you say and what you actually are telling people is not wide enough to attract much initial attention. Over the long haul, however, when you are trying to get to know someone, or to build a relationship with some-one, ambiguous communication will inevitably lead to difficulties. Both you and your long-term listener will detect the fact that you don't mean what you say, or that there are meanings nested inside of meanings, or that your meanings mean different things depending on your mood.

What you say, how you say it, and when you say it are all actions that reflect who you are. In the same way, the quality of your writing reflects the quality of your thinking. Learning to write effectively and correctly enhances your thinking. And learning to talk effectively enhances your identity as a student. Once recognized as a conflicted, manipulative, or ambiguous communicator, a person gets little trust from others. And the person crystallizes a powerful, though unspoken, reputation that will hinder his or her progress.

Your mood, personality style, and basic emotional functioning govern the way you talk. Few of us spend our time talking to ourselves, so the process is always complicated by the interaction of at least two personalities. If one of the personalities is an authority figure, and the other is an authority-less figure, then the interaction is fraught with opportunities for disaster. Because even authority figures have personalities, the interaction of your personality with a professor's can produce some very complex talk.

Professors and students frequently engage in troubled talk. They speak to each other and misspeak to each other in very complex ways for very, very complex reasons. The focus in *Merlin* is on the key ingredients in the college environment that shape success and failure in the art of "studenting." The ingredients are the people involved: students and professors. Chapter 1 outlined some basics about student styles, so we turn next to professors' styles.

Four Professor Types

The contributions of professors to miscommunication deserve their own hall of fame. One of the most important things *Merlin* can do for you is to arm you with the knowledge of professor types. I can describe why the flow of talk from each professorial personality is the way it is. In this way, you will be able to anticipate the diversity of styles you will meet and then act in your own best interests. Anticipation is a form of *Merlin-talk*, and it can be a powerful way to communicate. But to anticipate, you must have knowledge. Here are some professor personality styles that you are likely to encounter.

Arrogant Profs

Some professors think that they are national treasures like the Statue of Liberty. Their arrogance is usually based on some real achievements. But their perception of those achievements is distorted.

The arrogant professor is legendary. Recipients of an arrogant prof's communications would say "notorious." Talk flowing from an arrogant person is hurtful and noxious. *Noxious* means poisonous, and there is nothing more so than talk and behavior designed to intimidate the listener. The irony of an *educator* behaving arrogantly is usually lost on arrogant professors, who do not see themselves as educators but rather as intellectual rarities to whom the college should show appropriately lavish gratitude.

Central to the arrogant professor's personality is a belief, usually unconscious, that only by a forceful show of intellectual superiority will he or she be accepted, respected, and admired. At a deeper level, the arrogant person is insecure and inferior-feeling. Arrogance, especially the paradox of *intellectual* arrogance (if they are as smart as they think they are, shouldn't they be able to figure this out?), is really armor plate designed to protect the self-image from feelings of weakness and worthlessness.

Arrogance also stems from anger that cannot be expressed in simpler ways. An arrogant person is an angry person. He or she has learned to deal with other people hostilely, but the hostility is disguised. The reason for the disguise varies with different people. However, you can be sure that if talking to a person makes you feel intimidated, then that was the deliberate (but covert) intention of the talker.

In academia, many people are arrogant. Being nice to an arrogant professor appeases him or her only in the short run. Revealing how intimidated you feel works better. The smaller you become, the bigger the arrogant prof's self-image becomes. The prof feels great. You feel like weasel droppings.

A MEMO FROM MERLIN

☛ You can be sure you're talking to an ARROGANT prof if:

☆ just thinking about speaking with the person makes you anxious.

☆ you talk in complete sentences, and the prof talks in terse half-phrases and grunts that you don't understand but pretend you do.

☆ you cannot picture yourself buying a used car from this prof.

☆ you would very much like to sell a used car to this prof.

☆ you learn a great deal from this person, but it does not seem worth it.

Narcissistic Profs

Arrogant profs think they are national treasures. Narcissistic profs wish they could be. The difference between the two is the degree of certainty available to them. Narcissistic people behave grandiosely because they lack the bedrock certainty of the truly arrogant. Narcissists are besieged with self-doubts, and they do not act primarily from anger. Anger frightens them, because they lack the armor plate of the arrogant to protect them from its consequences.

Narcissistic profs act mostly from sadness (sometimes actual clinical depression) that they are struggling against. The self-image here is unprotected, very fragile, and easily wounded. To avoid wounds inflicted by other people, narcissists become overalert to what people think of them. Such hypervigilance to others' opinions serves the narcissist well as an early warning system. But emotional radar like this has a price. The narcissist can easily experience many "false alarms" and "detect" insult or slight where there is none. As a consequence, the narcissistic prof spends most of his or her energy repairing real or imagined wounds to self-esteem.

As a result, the narcissist is, of course, self-absorbed, self-focused, and narrowly attentive to self-interests. On the surface, the narcissistic prof appears much like the arrogant one, but there is a telltale difference: Narcissistic professors are hungry for love and acceptance, and therefore do not act to intimidate or alienate others.

Narcissistic professors are charming, witty, and challenging people. They do not like competition from their students. A bright student is a threat. An experienced student is a threat. A bright, experienced, and mature student is unbearable. (Adult learners, be wary!)

A MEMO FROM MERLIN

☛ You can be sure you're talking to a NARCISSISTIC prof if:

☆ after an interaction, you feel empty or strangely saddened.

☆ during a conversation, you find your mind wandering to images of peacocks, floral wallpaper, or gold-plated Cadillacs.

☆ the prof makes you feel as if you had done something mediocre—not bad, just "not up to par."

☆ his or her briefcase comes from Bloomingdale's.

☆ you can't picture the prof spending time alone, absorbed in some hobby or television program or other soothing activity.

Indifferent Profs

An indifferent professor is a person who you are not sure is real. Detached, cold, and aloof, the indifferent prof finds teaching more laborious than childbirth. Classroom style of the indifferent prof is chaotic, although it is rationalized as a liberating "laissez-faire" professional orientation. Students experience it as professional apathy.

The indifferent prof is never enthusiastic about anything. In fact, cynicism and intellectual nihilism are more likely to be associated with the detached style. It is as if, from the indifferent prof's viewpoint, nothing matters. There is no right and wrong, no priorities, no values, no real reason to teach anyone anything. Teaching is a job. The fact that it is other people who are the students is simply an ugly fact of life.

Warm and tender feelings are alien to the indifferent person. For some, these human emotions are quite frightening, so they are dismissed as immature or histrionic excesses. Interacting with students is a chore that is carried out as quickly and efficiently as possible. Curtness is the order of the day.

At some deeper level, the indifferent person is not at all the cool, restrained, detached intellectual he or she appears to be. Like the narcissist, the detached person is frightened of close contacts with others. Intimacy in any of its forms is anxiety provoking. As you might guess, this kind of personality style has a dark personal history, usually beginning in childhood experiences that were emotionally painful and disruptive.

The detached prof *has* to be removed from others, *has* to be cool and apparently uncaring, *has* to be withdrawn and professional. For only in these ways can the threat of close contact, of letting others see the real self, be warded off. If a person with this style of defense finds himself or herself in a position of authority (such as being a professor), then the focus becomes the "neutral" subject matter, rather than the people being taught.

Of course, subject matter is never neutral. Human ideas cannot be sterilized. So the whole unconscious strategy of emotional detachment is prone to abrupt and painful failure at various times in the indifferent person's life.

A MEMO FROM MERLIN

☛ You can be sure you're talking to an INDIFFERENT prof if:

☆ it feels as if you're talking to yourself.

☆ he or she keeps reading the newspaper during your advisement interview.

☆ the prof says things such as: "World War II culminated in the atomic bombing of two Japanese cities. It was a bad experience for the Japanese people."

   or: "Freud introduced the concept of childhood sexuality. People did not like his ideas."

   or: "The material for this course is interesting. Pay attention."

☆ can't remember your name after teaching you three courses in a row.

☆ keeps telling you how unimportant are large chunks of the readings he/she has assigned.

Students tend to feel ignored and rejected when they take a course with a detached professor or have one as an adviser. What they are actually being exposed to is a protective wall that does not yield to the human touch. And, consequently, they are unlikely to learn much that will enrich their sense of the human spirit.

Obsessive Profs

As Neil Simon made clear in *The Odd Couple,* this is a world of Felixes and Oscars. The obsessive prof is a Felix. Control over every detail of life is the obsessive person's passion. Felix-type professors are models of orderliness, organization, and exactness. They make clear to their students with thirty-page handouts the requirements for the course, the readings, the day on which one should read which book, the exact dates of all exams, the exact topic outline of every class through a fifteen-week semester, and the precise number of discussions, home-work assignments, and demonstrations that will occur throughout the course.

From the learner's point of view, especially for the beginning college student, this apparent precision is wondrous. After a while, it is overwhelming. After a small while longer, it is numbing. By the end of the semester, it is anger-provoking, for the student begins to feel smothered, blocked, and steered rather than taught.

The strengths of the obsessive prof are organization and attention to detail. Students will frequently feel as if every moment of their semester is planned and orchestrated. They will be right. But, ironically, all this planning and control actually produces confusion, resentment, and blocks learning. The apparent helpfulness of the obsessive prof's guides is illusion. A multitude of rules, regulations, guidelines, criteria, or whatever name the prof gives his or her attempts at control is stifling.

There is a real difference between exactitude and obsessiveness: *Exacting* profs are precise, clear, and flexible. *Obsessive* professors are pseudo-precise, scattered, and rigid. Any change in their plan causes anxiety and crankiness.

Students exposed to obsessive profs will frequently find themselves swamped with details that can't be synthesized into a meaningful whole. Despite the rules, guidelines, and handouts, students realize they are lost in a sea of information without an idea in sight.

CHAPTER TWO

The student's feeling of being swamped mirrors the cognitive style of the professor. Obsessive profs see the trees but can't find the forest. In clinical assessment, a psychologist will show a person a Rorschach ink blot that looks to most people like a pretty butterfly. The obsessive person sees little details of it, such as a dot that looks like Alfred Hitchcock's profile, or a tiny gray area that looks like a canoe. But the whole card, with this big, beautiful butterfly, is not seen until you call attention to it. And then the obsessive person will find it uninteresting.

In similar fashion, the obsessive prof focuses on the details of his or her subject matter, thereby losing the "big picture." There is no synthesis, no global meaningfulness, no clear conceptual map. For the student, the result is frustrating. This teaching style has been called, accurately I think, intellectual masturbation.

Can you find the profile of Alfred Hitchcock in this inkblot? If you can, why do you want to?

A MEMO FROM MERLIN

☛ You can be sure you're talking to an OBSESSIVE prof if:

☆ the prof does all the talking.

☆ he or she picks lint off your shirt during your conversation.

☆ prof carries his or her own box of blackboard chalk in case there's a shortage.

☆ when the course is over, your only clue to what it was about is the collection of handouts and tests you've kept.

☆ after the course, you've acquired a new habit: You argue with yourself.

CHAPTER TWO

The Significance of Knowing Professorial Types

You may be wondering how knowing about professor types can help you. Knowledge of this kind is valuable for two reasons:

- It permits you to identify and to anticipate the behavior of the important people you will study with. As discussed, anticipation permits you control.

- Knowing about the types of personalities you are likely to meet in the classroom or in faculty offices during advisement permits you to regulate your own behavior and change your expectations to meet the demands that will be made on you. Knowledge really is power.

There are several reasonable conclusions we can draw from knowledge about these various personality styles.

First, Merlin is not the place to provide an exhaustive listing of types even if such a list could be generated. The types presented here—*arrogant, narcissistic, indifferent,* and *obsessive*—are those personality styles that give students the most difficulty and stress in college. There are others, but knowing about these gives you the skill to identify others as you require.

Second, certain combinations of student personality type and professor personality type are like the Star Trek version of matter meeting antimatter. You can work these out by reviewing the Darwin, Damocles, and Merlin styles discussed in Chapter 1 and by contrasting them with the professor types discussed in this chapter. For example, imagine what would happen when a Darwin student meets up with a narcissistic prof. Or consider the catastrophe waiting to happen in the pairing of a Damocles with an obsessive prof. You see what I mean. Some examples of the three most painful combinations are given in Table 2.1

Table 2.1 The Three Worst Student-Professor Combinations

Student-Professor Match	Typical Outcomes
1. Damocles student with arrogant professor	Damocles is terrorized. Professor's self-esteem and feelings of power are enhanced. Student wilts. Professor expands.
	Damocles: "When Professor Despot asks me a question, he makes me want to curl up and die!"
	Professor Despot: "Most students are dead from the neck up."
2. Darwin student with narcissistic professor	Darwin dares esteemed professor to say something brilliant. Professor feels challenged to prove self. Student is combative. Professor is impressed with himself.
	Darwin: "Professor Florid thinks he's brilliant, but he's just a show-off."
	Professor Florid: "This student thinks I'm brilliant, which is pretty insightful for such a slow-witted person."
3. Damocles student with obsessive professor	Damocles is certain that whatever *can* go wrong *will* go wrong. Professor is certain that nothing can go wrong so long as everyone follows the rules, the rules about the rules, and the fundamental rule to keep track of the changes in rules that prevent things from going wrong.
	Damocles: "Professor Lintpicker knows what she's doing, but she wants so much from us, I can't keep up. I'm just not as smart as the other students. I just don't know what's going on."
	Professor Lintpicker: "This student is a rebel. She needs to learn how to be more organized and do it my way."

Third, in my experience the majority of professors fall into none of these extreme categories. Most student-professor combinations are not troublesome. But some are. It takes only one or two unanticipated experiences with the extreme types discussed here (and you *will* meet at least one of them at some time in your college career) to sour an otherwise productive intellectual environment. Knowing who's out there will not make coping with them easier. It *will* make you less likely to overgeneralize the sour experiences into self-imposed obstacles.

The Care and Feeding of Professors

Knowing the kinds of teachers you may meet gives you powerful control over your own actions. Accurate anticipation is 90 percent of effective action. What's needed now are some practical *Merlin* techniques designed to do two things:

• Lower your anxiety and frustration levels.

• Permit you to evade the obstacles embodied in each professor type.

In effect, you will learn to apply what you know about professor types to encourage each prof to teach you well. Psychologists, skilled managers, and administrators know that the most effective way to deal with individual differences is to look for what's best in a person while ignoring the troublesome features. Put another way, you can catch more flies with honey than with vinegar.

☆ ★ ☆
The Professors Respond

Student:	Will my term paper be graded on the writing, like, you know, spelling and grammar and things?
Arrogant prof:	What do you think?
Narcissistic prof:	What would the world think of me if I didn't hold you responsible for good writing?
Indifferent prof:	This isn't an English course.
Obsessive prof:	Let me think about that. As long as you follow the format I've given you, check the style manual too, you should be all right. But better check with me as you write it before your final draft. Then again, it's your responsibility to write clear, correct, concise, precise English, you know? However, if you don't produce good writing it will detract from your grade, probably, depending on whether you have followed directions. And be sure, by the way, to get the paper in by the due date I've given you, or you'll lose points for that.

☆ ★ ☆

The Care and Feeding of Arrogant Profs

Meeting an arrogant prof's anger with your own anger is *the* recipe for disaster. The Merlin student knows that the goal remains constant: educating yourself. The goal never is to meet arrogance with arrogance, nor to outdo an arrogant professor's rudeness. And the Merlin student never plays oneupmanship games. Here are some practical *nevers:*

- *Never* permit your own anger to be triggered by an arrogant person.

- *Never* forget that arrogance stems from a combination of uncontrolled angry feelings and deep insecurity. Arrogant people are not superior; they are vulnerable human beings trying to hide their vulnerability.

- *Never* believe that an arrogant prof's arrogance is equal to his or her stupidity. Arrogant people usually have some special talent or skill to be arrogant about.

Here are some positive Merlin *always:*

- *Always* meet arrogance with kindness and restraint. If you can't find it in your own generosity of spirit to be kind to people who unwittingly hurt you, then do it to confuse them. It's a small sabotage, but it is a *Merlin* sabotage.

- *Always* be appropriately respectful and focus on what the prof can teach you, which is probably a great deal.

- *Always* avoid taking classes from that prof again. Frustration tolerance is a good thing, but there's no need to turn it into masochism.

The Care and Feeding of Narcissistic Profs

Competition is the central danger in talking to a narcissistic prof. Such a professor is easily wounded by other people's failure to admire him. But it is also true that the narcissist can never be fully satisfied even when others offer their genuine admiration. These profs are in competition with the achievements of others and with their own last, best effort.

- *Never* ignore or snub a narcissistic prof. Wherever you see this person, go out of your way to say hello or somehow acknowledge his or her presence. It's easier to pretend you don't see the narcissist sometimes, but he or she sees you, and won't forget the slight.

- *Never* argue an intellectual point with a narcissistic professor. Although intellectual disputes are ordinarily desirable, with the narcissist they are counterproductive. Better approach: well-phrased questions to elicit more information or to expose one-sided ideas. In this way, you display to the narcissist your noncompetitive ignorance, and the narcissist feeds you.

- *Never* expect to feel emotionally refreshed or enriched by contact with a narcissist. Resign yourself to intellectual enrichment.

- *Always* maintain eye contact with narcissists. They need to be looked at. Really.

- *Always* be an attentive listener, and keep your own verbal contributions to an absolute minimum.

- *Always* keep in mind that the narcissist has a deep core of sadness. Despite the public image of liveliness, the narcissistic prof functions on the edge of exhaustion. Genuine kindness expressed to such a person is never forgotten, and will be repaid in unexpected ways.

- *Always* maintain firm personal boundaries and appropriate distance from the narcissist. Narcissistic people do not make good chums or buddies. If you move in too close, they are prone, metaphorically speaking, to bite. Friendliness, not intimacy, is the order of the day.

- *Always* be prepared for abrupt mood shifts from the narcissistic professor. Such people vacillate between apparent warmth and cold crankiness. If you're treated dramatically differently by a narcissistic prof from time to time, realize that it's not personal and usually not caused by anything you've done or said. Be a Merlin: Realize that mood shifts are more or less involuntary and reflect the narcissist's character style.

The Care and Feeding of Indifferent Profs

Of all the professor types, the indifferent prof is least likely to be able to teach you something. I do not mean to say that emotionally detached teachers are without value. I do mean that their value to the student is minimal and in many cases outweighed by negative consequences of their role modeling. Education depends on human interaction, shared enthusiasm, and strong emotional attachments. None of these qualities is available from the indifferent prof.

Talking with an indifferent prof is a rare event. It is typical for such teacher-student conversations to revolve around course business and routine details. Very little enrichment will come from indifferent profs, and such people, unless they were tenured at a time when they were less indifferent, do not last long in the teaching business.

Merlin students treat their experiences with indifferent profs realistically. That is to say, they work as hard as they ever do, but they recognize that a semester with such a teacher is more of an endurance test than an educational enterprise. There is little to be done, except for self-protective strategies that will guard you against the very contagious disease of apathy.

- *Never* look for the silver lining in this particular cloud. I do not know how to change indifferent people, and you, as a student, do not have time to try.

- *Never* allow yourself to succumb to feelings of apathy or detachment that you see being modeled by this kind of teacher. It is a very contagious malady. The cure is recognizing it and switching to another prof's course if possible.

- *Never* assume that the subject matter taught by this prof is as uninteresting or useless as he or she makes it seem. In skilled hands, any area of human ideas is rich, and sometimes exciting. Don't confuse the message with the messenger.

- *Never* conclude that there is something wrong with you—that, for instance, you are not smart enough or talented enough to really make sense of the subject matter. The deficiency here lies with the indifferent prof.

- *Always* look quickly for another course, another teacher in the same area and switch.

- *Always* rely on the texts and other reading materials the prof has required. They are unlikely to be indifferent, too. At least you can learn by exposure to the written ideas of other people in the same field.

- *Always* tell yourself, out loud if necessary, that indifference and detachment are defense mechanisms of a crippled personality. They are not ways of seeing the world, doing your work, or living your life.

The Care and Feeding of Obsessive Profs

Simple: Do what they ask.

Whereas the indifferent prof has the capacity to demoralize a student, the obsessive prof has the power to disappoint. Amid all the details, rules, guidelines, facts, the student has the expectation that something important is happening. This prof knows his or her business! By the end of the course, when it is very clear that nothing is clear, the student feels let down, cheated.

It is ironic that the obsessive prof, compared to the indifferent one, is enthusiastic about his or her area of knowledge. But the obsessive prof loses the meaningfulness of it in an effort to avoid ambiguity and surprise. What such efforts create is, expectably, uncertainty and confusion.

A Merlin student can nevertheless profit from exposure to such professors. Here again are some practical strategies:

- *Never* circumvent, change, or fail to follow the rules set down by the obsessive prof. No matter how unnecessary they seem, they do serve a function: They keep the obsessive professor happy.

- *Never* assume that the obsessive prof understands the main themes or implications contained in all the details any better than you do. They don't teach clear concepts, ideas, and themes because they don't see them.

- *Never* suffer in silent confusion. Voice your questions politely. Look for help from classmates who are also struggling to avoid intellectual indigestion.

- *Never* expect all the rules, due dates, and requirements presented in the first class to remain unchanged just because they appeared on handouts. They will change, and change, revert to the originals, and then change some more.

- *Never* miss classes. *Never. Never.*

- *Always* abide by the currently operative rule, due date, or requirement.

- *Always,* when uncertain about how something should be done, ask the prof for clarifying information. You will get more than you bargained for, but at least you won't violate any rules. And the prof will learn to respect you because you care about the details.

- *Always* work at synthesizing, integrating, simplifying information to squeeze from it the main ideas, themes, and concepts.

- *Always* remember that the obsessive prof cares about what he or she is teaching—perhaps too much. But if you can't learn anything else from this prof, this lesson is a satisfactory one.

The Reality of Teaching in College

There is a risk in describing the extreme types of troublesome teachers. In our focus on the character flaws of a few, we may lose sight of many people who function daily to educate their students despite pressures and privations not found in other professions. We will say more about the "good" teacher (the Merlin prof) in the next section.

Who College Teachers Are

College teachers are people who have spent a great deal of their adult lives pursuing advanced knowledge and skill in largely academic settings. Most college teachers, but not all, have earned doctoral degrees (Ph.D., Ed.D., Psy. D.) in a particular subject area.The average doctoral degree takes at least four years of full-time postcollege study, and some doctorates take considerably longer. As part of the process, the Ph.D. candidate must also produce a full-scale piece of scholarly research, called a doctoral dissertation, that meets stringent standards of scholarship. Some doctoral degrees are also associated with lengthy internship requirements, such as those in clinical and counseling psychology. To top off the requirements, a good percentage of newly graduated Ph.D.s elect to spend one or more years in postdoctoral specialty studies as part of their professional development. Prestigious universities that offer good jobs in academia want Ph.D.s with this kind of extensive education history. But the salaries that are offered to well-trained Ph.D.s in academia are substantially lower than the salaries earned by equivalently educated people in other professions, and their prestige is lower than that of, say, a physician or a lawyer.

Why They Do It

Why do they do it? There are at least two answers to the question, one of them apparently cynical and one of them not. But both are probably true in differing proportions for different profs.

The first reason is that the typical Ph.D. in a liberal arts area such as English, history, philosophy, or language has few things, other than teaching, he or she can do. Playwright George Bernard Shaw is credited with the cynical witticism "Those who can't do, teach." Teaching these areas is a primary activity that follows from expertise in them. It is true that an English professor might write novels or plays, but the commercially successful author is the exception. A person with a Ph.D. in languages might work as a translator, but teaching language or the literature of that language is more likely to be a major full-time activity if the person wants to eat and pay rent. In a real way for some teachers, Shaw was right. They must teach.

Yet unlike Shaw, we have to ask the more primary question: Why then do some people choose to study intellectual areas and spend years preparing themselves in such areas if they can "do" little more than teach others? And college teachers are not naive: they know that teaching earns less respect and less money than other pursuits. The answer, as simplistic as it sounds, is that they are intellectually engaged by their academic disciplines. Or, even more simply put, college

profs love their subjects, first and foremost. It may be intellectual love, but for most, it is just as passionate as romantic love. And the one thing that it is not is cynical. When you're done or almost done with your college education, these last two statements will probably make more sense. There are, however, two consequences that follow from this line of reasoning.

First, college profs are more likely to be focused on their subject matter than on their students. They are, by and large, scholars, not counselors, not social workers, not substitute parents. They love their intellectual pursuits and they wish their students would too, but it is not essential. They are likely, therefore, to care less about the *technique* of introducing others to their discipline than they care about the discipline itself. Not a good springboard for the traditional conception of a teacher. But it is nevertheless reality—for *some* college professors.

The second consequence that flows from the scholarly tradition of most college profs is that the vast majority have not spent any of their long classroom time learning how to teach! Their training is typically in their subject areas—history, philosophy, psychology, business, and so on—*not* in how to teach students. Worse still, college teachers tend to teach as they have last been taught. And their last experience of teaching was graduate school, not college or high school. What sometimes appears to be arrogance, indifference, or lack of direction from new Ph.D.s in the classroom is more likely a reflection of that person's most recent personal educational experience. They simply don't remember what it was like to be an undergraduate! And no one has compelled them to learn how to teach because the Ph.D.s' teachers were concerned with *their* students' scholarly mastery, research skills, and capacity for independence, not their pedagogical development.

To make life just a little more difficult, the college teacher, on the job, has to produce constantly: publish papers, seek research grants, serve on institutional committees, publish papers, advise students, publish papers, and work to become tenured. If a college teacher does not meet the standards of his or her institution for tenure within the first few years of employment, his or her employment is terminated. Tenure almost always involves demonstrating intellectual productivity: Need I say it? Publishing papers. Note that excellence in teaching students is not necessarily a part of the tenure and promotion rat race at most colleges. Where does that leave you?

HARE-BRAINED IDEA I

It should leave you wiser and more prepared to understand who your teachers will be and what they are trying to do. You can learn from them the love of things intellectual, the willingness to do hard thinking, and the freedom that intellectual independence brings. But you need to bring with you some capacity to see your teachers as human beings moved by feelings and urges that do not necessarily coincide with your wishes. You should understand that your teachers' values may or may not be compatible with your needs for security, safety, and ease. And not because they are intellectually arrogant S.O.B.s, but because college profs are a product of a particular set of life experiences.

There is one further fact you should be aware of. Some college teachers, despite Shaw's cynical barb, can "do" other things, but don't. Physicists, mathematicians, psychologists, chemists, sculptors, to name just a few, teach college because they enjoy *teaching*. They may also pursue other professional interests simultaneously, but they *teach* because they derive satisfaction from sharing their expertise with students. In short, neither money nor lack of alternate professional avenues nor unwillingness to "work in the real world" is responsible for this kind of college teacher's teaching. He or she teaches because he or she loves teaching. They are few in number, but they are not rare.

About Merlin Profs

Experienced educators and administrators (even psychologists) know that if you want to find out who the good teachers in a school are, you ask the students.

Some faculty hate this idea. They argue that students are a class of human beings who do not yet have the knowledge or experience to judge professors accurately. What this argument is missing is the simple truth that, in fact, students are the most experienced "consumers" or "users" of teaching. That's what students do: get taught.

It is true that one or a handful of students may not be accurate judges of teaching talent in every sphere. But when the majority of students identifies a particular teacher as a "good" one, it is a denial of reality to assume that they are engaged in mass delusion.

In truth, I do not know all the qualities that make a good teacher. I know some of the outstanding qualities that make for effective education and student satisfaction. You probably have your own list, and if you don't, you should think about creating one.

For now, here are the identifiable qualities of the Merlin professor:

• Merlin professors have expert knowledge of their subject matter. Besides possessing the usual academic credentials, an "expert" is a practitioner of the knowledge he or she teaches. Thus an art teacher usually is also an artist; an art historian researches the history of art; a psychologist practices psychology or operates as a researcher.

The point is that the status of "expert" means active involvement in the discipline. Such involvement reflects commitment and passion for the subject: a very good sign.

It might interest you to know that "expert" status is the rationale behind the "publish or perish" policy that governs hirings and firings in academia. Despite the abuses of this standard, it is generally true that a practitioner of an intellectual discipline is involved in researching or sharing new knowledge through direct performance or through writing that is exposed to the scrutiny and criticism of professional peers.

(If Merlin were forced to pick one and only one characteristic of a good prof, it would be *expert knowledge in his or her subject.* Everything else should follow from this central feature. Many, many educators, administrators, and psychologists disagree with this assessment of good teaching. Sorcerers are too old and cranky to give disagreement much weight.)

• Merlin professors remember vividly their own studenting. They can see things the way a student sees them. They know what it is like to learn at various phases in your life. With great empathy, they are able to envision what things look like to you when you are exposed to them for the first time. Despite their own expertise, they never forget what it takes to approach new ideas as a beginner.

THE CARE AND FEEDING OF PROFESSORS

• Merlin profs have a genuine interest in and affinity for new learners. It gives Merlin profs pleasure to see students think for the first time about ideas they have introduced. They are not indifferent, rarely narcissistic, and never arrogant. Although, like most people, they will experience hard times in their lives that affect their performance in the classroom, they will generally be consistently Merlinesque in their warmth, affability, and graciousness.

• Merlin profs model excellence in both intellectual pursuits and in personal relationships. They treasure the life of the mind. They do not make students feel ignored, put down, or inept because they are beginners.

Instead, they make students understand what needs to be learned, what skills that will take, and then they provide models of how to do it. They hold themselves and their students to *realistically* high standards of performance.

Realistic is the critical adjective. A Merlin prof does not expect his or her students to learn what he or she has not been taught. These profs want you to learn what they are teaching. When one method does not work, they'll try another. Their belief is that there is always another way, and that their students are people for whom it is worth designing and redesigning learning strategies.

• Merlin profs are exacting without being obsessive. They have given a great deal of thought to their lectures, discussions, and demonstrations. And it shows. In their precision and in the intellectual demands they make on students, they are leaders, not taskmasters. They will reach out a hand to pull you up. They will pause for you to catch up. But they will never push you forward.

Such teachers exude an air of knowing their stuff, and, in fact, that's how students usually describe them. Students point out that these profesors are demanding in a challenging rather than intimidating way. Such teachers' competence in their subject matter is so obvious without being pretentious that students want to imitate them.

These teachers expect topflight work, but, more important, Merlin profs have confidence in each student's capacity to produce it. Sometimes the prof will be wrong. But he or she prefers to err on the side of believing in a student's competence rather than searching for the student's limitations. Positive expectations communicated as though they were routine make a big difference in the way you feel about yourself—and about the subject matter.

• Merlin profs, like their academic counterparts, Merlin students, are gentle. The gentleness is noticeable in their genuine warmth toward other people, in their sensitivity to a student's needs, and in their eagerness to share their thoughts without imposing them on you.

The teachers you will remember ten, fifteen, or twenty years after you leave college will not be the arrogant ones (except at parties for a good laugh). Nor will you remember the obsessive ones. You will remember the teachers who touched your life by demanding much of you and having the confidence that you would meet the demands.

Some Summary, Some Conclusions

☆ Talking or writing reveals you. A person's feelings, conflicts, and mood shape what he or she says and hears.

☆ Talking to professors takes some skill if you want to get the very best from them. Such skill is based on knowing the psychology of the personality types you will meet. In this chapter you saw these types of professor:

- Arrogant (angry)

- Narcissistic (self-protective)

- Indifferent (detached)

- Obsessive (rigid)

☆ Merlin profs are those teachers you will remember for a lifetime because they touched you with their expertise, their confidence in you, their leadership, and their gentleness.

Merlin wasn't always a sorcerer.
He flunked out of beauticians' school.

About This Chapter

Main Theme of the Chapter

A college diploma by itself does not make you employable.
Think of college as a process during which you acquire wisdom
about the art of learning, coping with obstacles, and navigating
through interpersonal relationships.

Related Ideas

What should you major in? A classic question with a nonclassic
answer: the Basic Information to Choose Honestly list.

☆ Past successes and failures?

☆ People, idea, or thing orientation?

☆ Happiest spending your time fantasizing about?

CHAPTER 3

So You Have to Major in Something

Choosing your major area of study is much like watching the hunter who shot Bambi's mother drive off a cliff in your new Mercedes sport coupe. "Mixed emotions" is probably an understatement.

Mixed emotions are common in selecting an area of study that is likely also to be a lifelong career choice. Students expect that earning a degree in a subject will provide them with a means of earning a living. This is certainly a sensible expectation, but it puts unwarranted pressure on the student at the time of choice. Such an expectation also places unrealistic constraints on the process of education. In the main, colleges cannot provide professional or vocational training. They can provide something more valuable.

A college education can help guide you toward a professional pathway or to make decisions about your life realistically. Without college, you will not enter medical or law school, most graduate schools, and very few executive training programs. But earning the relevant college degree does not make you a lawyer, doctor, accountant, teacher, psychologist, or corporate manager. It makes you a college graduate: that is, a person who is prepared and sufficiently skilled to learn more advanced skills in some more specialized area.

College is a necessity, but by itself, not sufficient preparation for any contemporary career or apprenticeship in the business community. There are a few exceptions, such as if you:

- inherit a family fortune or business

- have Nobel prize–winning writing talent

- dance like Pavlova

- paint like Monet

- compose like Beethoven

- have some anatomical variant that people will pay money to view.

The B.I.T.C.H. List

An enormous quantity of advice is available on how to choose your major. But the simple truth is that most students select their primary area of study on the basis of gut reactions. They know what feels right, and they have a general idea about the kinds of things that interest them and a realistic estimation of their abilities.

No one can tell you what major to select with any degree of certainty that it is right for you. More important, you should not believe for a moment that your selection is in any way final. Having chosen to major in English, for example, does not preclude also majoring in philosophy or psychology or biology at a later date or even simultaneously. Double majors are becoming more common, and students who return to college to major in a new discipline after obtaining their degrees are, if not commonplace, at least not so rare as was once the case.

So choosing a major does not mean you are trapped. It is not an ultimate decision. It is not a cosmic choice. It is not final. But you should know that, made wisely, choice of a major area of study can facilitate building the kind of life that will provide enduring satisfaction, financial success, and personal esteem. After all, college is worth something.

So how, you ask, do you do it? *How do you decide?* "I, too, want enduring satisfaction, financial success and personal esteem!" The best answer to your question is to give you a Merlin checklist of questions to ask yourself: the Basic Information to Choose Honestly list, or B.I.T.C.H. for short.

Basic Information to Choose Honestly
(The B.I.T.C.H List)

1. What is my academic history?

• Overall pattern of grades _____

• Types of courses I succeeded in _____

• College board scores _____

• Overall high school average _____

2. How do I spend my time when free to choose?

• People-oriented activities: Yes ☐ No ☐

• Thing-oriented activities: Yes ☐ No ☐

• Idea-oriented activities: Yes ☐ No ☐

3. In imagination or fantasy, what makes me happiest?

(check as many as apply)

• Great wealth   ☐

• Great power   ☐

• Respect and admiration from others   ☐

• Being more knowledgeable than others   ☐

• Unlimited sexual partners   ☐

• Serving others in some professional helping capacity   ☐

• The big four: wealth, power, admiration, and sex   ☐

Academic History

The purpose of the questions under this heading in the checklist should be obvious. Selection of a satisfactory major has to be based on a realistic assessment of your academic abilities. It's not much fun dreaming about being a doctor if you know that biology, chemistry, and physics are beyond your capacities or in conflict with your interests. On the other hand, little personal profit is to be gained from setting your sights on a career in hotel management when you know that wrestling with mathematical equations and spending hours in the physics lab make you nearly euphoric.

Truth hurts. Look at your high school grades. Examine the pattern of courses you took (or the pattern of courses you're taking if you're in college already). A good advisor does the same thing (and the admissions committee at your college does this religiously). Be your own best adviser.

Your history—the pattern of what you have actually done in academic situations—is the best predictor of what you can do with success and with satisfaction in the present. An honest answer to the history part of the B.I.T.C.H. list can reveal the pattern of your strengths and weaknesses. For some students, the strengths will shine through, whereas for others, the weaknesses will be most salient.

Truth hurts. Yet truth is a powerful tool for taking control of your life. When you've answered the history questions for yourself, you won't need an academic adviser to tell you whether nuclear physics, pre-med, pre-law, philosophy, or symbolic logic are feasible options for you. *You* will know.

A warning: You are not trapped by your history. Even if your pattern of grades and achievements in the past was mediocre or poor, it does not guarantee continued mediocrity in college. In fact, a self-examination of this kind may actually help you to alter the future.

Moreover, for reasons I cannot explain, even the poorest of students in high school sometimes blossoms in college. Perhaps it is the newfound freedom, or the influence of good teachers, or the pressure from peers and parents. Or perhaps it is merely the passage of time: college students are chronologically older and more experienced than they were in high school. Whatever the reason, people change if they decide to do so.

People, Things, Ideas

Some years ago, psychologist Anne Roe attempted to classify people's choices of careers by whether they were thing-oriented or people-oriented. She developed an elaborate theory based on ideas from Freud's psychoanalysis and from Abraham Maslow's humanistic psychology. Roe tried to explain the differences between people-centered jobs (doctors, teachers, psychologists) and thing-oriented jobs (auto mechanics, electrical engineers) in terms of the unconscious needs presumably gratified by the type of career chosen. (I've often wondered how Roe would account for careers such as embalmer, oral surgeon, and taxidermist, but questions such as these make for worry lines.)

You might want to consult Richard Nelson Bolles's *What Color Is Your Parachute?* (annually revised since 1972; current edition is 1989, from Ten Speed Press, Berkeley, California), where job hunting is the context for applying Roe's ideas about people orientations and thing orientations.

Bolles provides several self-rating instruments and exercises to help his readers classify themselves and match their preferences to potential job choices. However, this best-selling book navigates between pop psychology and practical self-help without attention to the important shades of gray that lie between the seemingly clear-cut blacks and whites.

Roe's theory did not survive the scientific tests to which psychologists exposed it over the years. It was too simplistic, and far removed from the facts of real vocational choices. But the basic concept of people-oriented and thing-oriented careers has evolved into a vocational counseling tool that some psychologists and vocational counselors use to help people know themselves and to narrow their decisions to realistic sets of choices. To make Anne Roe's picture slightly more complete, it is necessary to add the concept of idea-oriented people to those who are person- or thing-oriented.

HARE-BRAINED IDEA II: PUNK

The trouble with categorical approaches such as these is they imply that placement in one category excludes placement in any other. Reality being what it is, people generally fit into more than one category at a time. It was the implicit notion of mutually exclusive categories that finally subverted Roe's original theory. A more logically acceptable strategy is to view these concepts as dimensions rather than as pigeonholes. From the dimensional viewpoint, it is clear that everyone has *some* capacity for all three orientations, with one of them dominating a person's style and preferences. But all people exhibit in different situations varying degrees of freedom to express their strongest preference.

It might help to think of the three orientations as dimensional rating scales from zero to ten, *with each person occupying a point on all three scales simultaneously.* It might be visualized like the scales in Figure 3-1. I should point out that the scales illustrated here are merely hypothetical models of the interaction of several variables at once.

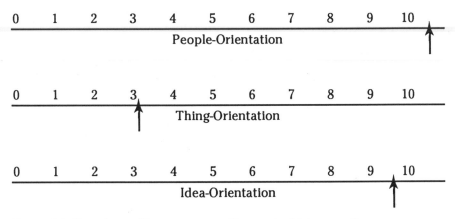

Figure 3.1 Hypothetical Dimensions in Choosing a Major or a Career
The arrows in each of the dimensions indicate the strength of a hypothetical person's preferences. Illustrated here is the profile I imagine characterizes students interested in psychology, education, and nursing, to name just a few people-oriented majors with substantial intellectual content to them. A different profile would characterize students interested in physics, mathematics, law, and philosophy. Try your own "thought experiment."

SO YOU HAVE TO MAJOR IN SOMETHING

Think of this model of intellectual or vocational preference as a "thought experiment" in the spirit of physicists Galileo and Albert Einstein and psychologist Kurt Lewin. A thought experiment is just a mental simulation, an act of intellectual curiosity and creativity. Thought experiments are designed to provoke "what if?" questions that can be answered only by real experiments. As Merlin himself understood, first you have to create the questions.

Figure 3.1 shows the relationship among the three orientations for a student who I imagine in my thought experiment is spontaneously interested in people and in ideas, but has little affinity for working with or exploring things. This thought experiment raises intriguing questions.

Suppose, for example, the profile shown in the figure had the idea orientation at 9.5 and the people orientation at 7.5. Would we still have a student interested in majoring in psychology or education? Probably. But the interest would center on research psychology or educational research rather than on clinical psychology or classroom teaching.

The point, of course, is that the three dimensions interact and permit one to ask "Where do my preferences lie?" *and* "How strong is each of them?" *and*, assuming I can answer these questions, "How do my preferences accord with the major areas of college study?"

Try to characterize yourself in terms of these hypothetical dimensions. Be aware as you do so that it is unlikely that these three dimensions constitute the complete basis for choosing a major you will be satisfied with. But the dimensions can simplify and clarify the process if you use them in concert with the knowledge you gain from the remaining items in the B.I.T.C.H. checklist. Here are some characteristics associated with each of the orientations.

People Orientation

- Empathy for others: that is, an ability to understand what other people are thinking and feeling and sufficient interest to care.

- Curiosity about what people do, how they do it, and how to help them do it.

- Desire to spend free time socializing with others, pursuing group rather than solitary activities.

- Tendency to learn best when subject matter focuses on human relevance, when working with a human teacher rather than with textbooks, computer terminals, or laboratory apparatus.

Thing Orientation

- Satisfaction from knowing how things work, how to keep them working smoothly, performing your own repairs.

- Curiosity about technological advances in computers, electronics, photography equipment, complex automobiles and engines, stereo equipment as important as the music it plays.

- Ability to "think with your hands." That is to say, you work well with your hands, building, creating, carpentering, drawing, performing, fixing.

- Ease in restoring things to working condition or spending hours on a private hobby involving building things or collecting things and organizing them.

- Preference for showing yourself to others through the things you make or do rather than face to face.

Idea Orientation

- Greatest pleasures are reading, talking, and writing about ideas.

- Natural affinity for synthesizing facts and concepts into memorable wholes.

- Satisfaction from understanding how other people have solved problems or puzzles, with interest in applying solutions to new problems.

- Admiration for the great thinkers, such as Plato, Einstein, Woody Allen.

- Preference for leisure activities that center on diary keeping, fiction writing, science-fiction writing/reading, moviegoing.

- Ability and willingness to communicate ideas to others: "the natural teacher."

- Deliberate daydreaming or creatively using your fantasies to make daily living more exciting or livable.

Overview: The Corresponding Academic Majors

All three orientations can be present simultaneously in people. The key is to understand how they interact inside you. Many complex psychological diagnostic procedures could be used to help you find out. But in my experience, the average student has sufficient self-knowledge to answer the important questions without major psychological intervention. Which orientation is strongest in you?

- **People major:** Your choice has to permit contact and interaction with human beings. Social science, the fine arts and the performing arts, and education are areas to consider first.

- **Thing major:** Your choice should center on learning the skills you will need to interact with or create new technologies. Natural and physical sciences, some arts, and some parts of experimental psychology will be attractive.

- **Idea major:** Your choice has to be qualified by how much people orientation you also have. If there's sufficient interest in people, then human service fields should appeal to you. If you're more idea-oriented than people-oriented, then the sciences and philosophy await with beckoning arms.

The point, of course, is that choosing a major is a personal event that can be accomplished only if you are open with yourself. Armed with some rudimentary knowledge about people, things, and ideas, you have a better than average chance of selecting the field in which you will find satisfaction and enduring emotional and intellectual engagement.

 M

Dear Undecided:

Choosing a major is NOT like buying a new car. It can't be traded in for a new one when it wears out. Your major is very much a part of you. You can have more than one, and you can grow beyond the limits of your studies. But the growth is IN you.

Agriculturally yours,

Merlin

Doing the Major

When you learned to drive a car for the first time, or to ride a bicycle successfully, you did something that until then you could not describe from firsthand experience. But now, you have a kind of knowledge about driving cars or riding bicycles that someone who has not yet done these things cannot have. There is value in knowing *about* driving cars and *about* riding bicycles, but there is wisdom in *driving* and *riding*.

In an analogous way, *majoring* in a subject gives you a kind of wisdom, not just about the subject but in the process of majoring, in the art of confronting emotional and intellectual obstacles. You practice social, intellectual, and emotional *knowing* that someone who has not done the major cannot practice. It is the Merlin art of studenting.

Merlin has been asked frequently to define these wisdoms that come from the art of studenting. There was a time when he used to try to do that. He thought he could define this process clearly and operationally. But his own experiential knowledge in this area has grown to the point that Merlin recognizes he cannot define "studenting wisdom" in a way that will satisfy most people. He knows that it happens. He knows that it will happen for you. He even knows how to recognize it when he sees it in a Merlin student. But the description of the process given above is about as concrete and clear as Merlin knows how to be.

It's like Zen. If Merlin really understood how to communicate the concept, it would not be the concept. Sorry. Merlin is not fond of mysticism. But he's learned to tolerate ambiguity when he senses that something important would be lost. Hope you can too. It will be the biggest payoff on your investment.

CHAPTER THREE

Satisfaction with Self

What makes you happiest in your fantasy? The last item in the B.I.T.C.H. checklist alerts you to one of the variables that is most likely responsible for long-term satisfaction with your major: satisfaction with yourself.

Choosing a major also means selecting an area of intellectual engagement that is compatible with your view of who you are. What are your fantasies, when you really let yourself go? Wealth? Power? Superior knowledge? Three acrobats and a jar of peanut butter? *What?*

If sex, money, or power are part of your fantasies, you are normal. Disgustingly normal. But you also need to get real. If you can honestly say to yourself that factor X is what makes you happiest, then factor X and nothing else will do as you plan your life. Majoring in education will not lead to wealth. Pursuing a career in philosophy is not likely to bring you to the heights of power. Your common sense must play a part in your choices.

In truth, the people, thing, and idea classification is the best way to make these decisions. Check your fantasies for what they reveal about your personal orientation. You may discover that your sexual fantasies are really strivings for intimacy and warmth and love (and that requires *people*).

Or perhaps your dreams of great wealth and power reveal at their core a need to be in control of your life through knowledge (and that is likely an *idea* orientation). But above all, be real. Be honest with yourself. And you will be satisfied with your choice of major. No matter what the neighbors think.

Some Summary, Some Conclusions

☆ Earning your college degree by itself is not a final step in your preparation for life. It can be the ticket to further professional or graduate training or to apprenticeship in the business community.

☆ Choosing your major is usually an emotionally intense experience, which can be lessened if you realize that it is not a *final* decision.

☆ Honesty with yourself should permit you to decide whether you are people oriented, thing oriented, or idea oriented.

☆ There is a wisdom that comes from "majoring" in itself that permits you to grow emotionally and cognitively beyond what subject matter is learned. Your major is really a part of you, even if you grow beyond it.

☆ The Merlin student majors in a subject to get an education, not just a diploma.

Someone once called Merlin "cute." She's doing eternity as an Edsel.

About This Chapter

Main Theme of the Chapter

Some teachers and advisors have to be taught the art of teaching and advising by students. Apathy, burnout, personal distress, and sheer incompetence are, in part, responsible for poor teaching and advising. The Merlin student actively assists teachers and advisers to teach and advise with enthusiasm and vitality. This Merlin technique is called *appropriately sensitive schmoozing* (acronym optional).

Related Ideas

Executing a skillful schmooze requires:

☆ Personal control over anger and sarcasm

☆ Anticipation and planning

☆ Gentle humor

☆ Active rather than passive responsibility

CHAPTER 4

Getting Them to Teach and Advise You

Teachers teach. Advisers advise. Students student. This is the way of the world.

If you are prepared to student, it is very frustrating to be paired with a teacher who does not teach. Frustration stems from the powerless role in which students function relative to professors. Can you imagine yourself saying to a prof who gives one boring, empty class after another for a semester, "Excuse me, Professor Deadwood, but you cannot teach to save your life or mine. Why don't you become a dentist so that people who expect pain can have their expectations confirmed?"

I cannot imagine saying this when I was a student (nor could I imagine saying this now to a colleague in my role as chairman of a department). I can fantasize about doing it, but I can also envision the consequences. The fantasy gets sweaty and ends abruptly at that point. But it *is* satisfying. (Merlin secret: Use fantasy to satisfy otherwise objectionable wishes. Just don't tell anyone.)

Unfortunately, fantasy by itself does not change reality. To make those changes, one has to learn the Merlin art of *appropriately sensitive schmoozing*. The Merlin definition of *schmoozing* is the "art of diplomatic questioning with humor and respect."

The Merlin Art of Schmoozing

Skillful Merlin schmoozing is goal-oriented communication for coping with relatively competent but distracted or indifferent people. A properly executed schmooze will not enable an incompetent person suddenly to function competently, but it will work wonders with a competent professional who, for his or her own reasons, is not currently functioning at peak levels.

For our purposes, there are two situations in college that are ripe for the application of intelligent schmoozing: the classrooms of boring and bored professors who have a lot to teach students but have forgotten how, and the offices of advisers who don't put much energy into advising.

Four Boring Types

There are so many reasons some professors are boring that to enumerate them all would bore you. Here are some of the common ones you are likely to experience, if you can recognize them:

- **Novice teachers** who have been in the classroom only a short time since completing graduate training (or who are still in graduate training). They have only half their attention on teaching, with the other half devoted to finishing their own work. Or, fresh from graduate school, without sufficient experience with undergraduates, they forget what it was like to be a college student. They teach you the way they were last taught: that is, like what they experienced in graduate school. *Novice teachers are boring or inefficient because they don't yet know what they are doing.*

- **Burned-out career teachers** who have been in the classroom over twenty years, have become fatigued, and see teaching as numbingly routine. *They are boring because they are bored.*

- **Impaired master teachers** who know what they are doing, love their subject matter, and love teaching, but who abruptly change for the worse. Most likely they are temporarily distressed by personal or health problems. Whatever the reasons for the abrupt change, they are not trivial but, you hope, temporary. *Be a Merlin: Give this kind of professor the benefit of the doubt.*

- **Incompetent twits** who are the living embodiments of George Bernard Shaw's dictum "Those who can't do, teach." These "teachers" typically don't know much about their subject matter despite graduate training, have no sensitivity to other people, do not care to learn how to teach, and blame students for not learning.("They're so dumb," or "Students are so immature," or "My students have such short attention spans.") *They are boring and inefficient in the classroom because they do not belong there, are dimly aware that they are in alien territory, but are ill prepared to do anything else.* Finesse does not work with these people. Avoid them.

Executing the Classroom Schmooze

Merlin goal: To get an education while you cope with boredom or inefficiency. You assist the professor in being a better teacher.

- Rev up your sense of humor. Be sure you are in control of your angry feelings. Look at the picture on your college ID card to put you in the proper frame of mind.

- Prepare thoughtful questions related to the material under study in your class. Such questions work better if they are conceptual rather than requests for factual information.

HARE-BRAINED
IDEA III :
"IVY LEAGUE"

    For example, here is a *poor* schmooze:

    "Professor Deadwood, what are the structures in the brain that make up the limbic system?"

    Professor D. is not encouraged by such questions to do any real teaching. He or she can merely refer you to previous lectures if this concept has already been discussed, or to a text where you are presumed to have read the material.

More skillful schmooze:

"Professor Deadwood, you might think this is a foolish question, but suppose we could control the limbic system with drugs? Do you think it would be possible to program a person's feelings with pills?"

This Merlin-inspired schmooze has three virtues:

1. It is stated disarmingly and plainly.

2. It is a request for an *application* of material taught that provides a professor with an opportunity to use his or her intelligence and expertise—and this outcome is the reason both of you are in the classroom.

3. It is a gentle invitation to humor in the service of intellectual exploration for both the professor and for the other students present, whose minds will generate all sorts of ideas from a question such as this one.

The skillfully executed schmooze provides some structure for teachers who otherwise have abandoned structure in favor of mindless routine. Schmoozing takes preparation on your part; if you are unwilling to take the time or spend the effort, you are not entitled to complain that your teacher "doesn't do anything." Even if your well-prepared schmooze has little positive effect on the teacher's teaching, it will have still served in educating *you.*

The skillful classroom schmooze is the best cure there is for un-stimulated, jaded, apathetic teachers. I have seen really artful student schmoozing bring educators' corpses back to life. (This maneuver is known, of course, as the "Lazarus Schmooze." There is also the "Mercy Schmooze" and the classic "Waterloo Schmooze." However, you will have to use your imagination to work these out for yourself.)

Appropriately sensitive schmoozing communicates interest and effort to teachers. They are rejuvenated, their faith in the art of teaching restored. Worthless semesters can be salvaged in this way, discoveries in the power of human communication can be made and knowledge gained. By practicing the Merlin art of studenting, you may restore the professor's art of teaching.

Merlin Schmoozing: Illustrative Do's and Don'ts

Don't Say	Do Say
"Professor von Twit, I didn't understand a word of what you were talking about last class. Could you repeat it?" *(Implies prof is confused or stupid.)*	"Professor von Twit, I can't help thinking about what you said in last class: Is it possible that some people even today act like the people in Plato's cave allegory and don't want to face new ideas?"
"Professor Valium, you go too fast with the codes for the programs. I'm not a computer. Could you slow down?" *(Implies prof is insensitive boob.)*	"Professor Valium, sometimes I can't remember how to tie my own shoelaces, let alone remember all the code commands to write my computer program. Do you use any tricks or shortcuts to remember the commands?"
"Professor MacLethargy, this Melville story you assigned makes no sense. Is there any point to this?" *(Implies prof hasn't read it or does not care if irrelevant work is done.)*	"Professor MacLethargy, I'm having some trouble with the assigned reading. I wish I could figure out what Melville was doing in the 'Bartleby' story. I know there's something important going on, but I just can't see it."

Schmoozing Beyond the Classroom

Much of your college experience happens outside the classroom. In some ways, interactions with administrators, academic advisers, and supervisors are as important as student-teacher interactions. Many of the same rules apply to these experiences as apply to schmoozing a recalcitrant teacher.

CHAPTER FOUR

An academic adviser serves as combination disciplinarian, supervisor, and master-worker to whom you are apprenticed. On the face of it, your academic adviser helps you plan your academic career, including what courses to take, completing college or university requirements, and applying to graduate school. But in reality, advisers are much more.

At their best, advisers really are mentors. They teach you how to monitor your own progress, they stimulate you to dream of things you might never have thought of without their example, and they know how to help you through the tough times.

A good adviser may not be a psychologist, but he or she knows how to help you find one if that is appropriate. A good adviser is not a substitute mother or father, but he or she knows how to listen, when to shut up, when to negotiate, when to be firm in your best interests.

At their worst, advisers are the people who sign your registration forms once or twice a year. You are not eager to see them at any other time, and they are pleased that you are not eager. Most of what you learn about majoring in your chosen field you find out from other students or by reading the college catalog (which is usually wrong and outdated). And both you and your adviser collude to protect this system of advisement robotics.

If a student accepts robotic advisement, he or she is being robbed. When professors and deans permit the robotized process of twice-yearly form signings, they are thieves. But in this case, both thief and victim are impoverished by the crime.

The correction is not an obvious one. Experience predicts that faculty and administrators will talk about this problem forever, and form several committees to study the matter. Committees will make their reports to *advise* the deans, faculty, and president of the college.

The practical outcome of this advice?

Faculty, deans, and college presidents get to have more meetings, write more memos, and file more paper.

Simpler solution: *Students have to teach faculty and deans how to advise.* Appropriately sensitive schmoozing is the indicated treatment.

BRUCE VON BEETHOVEN, YOUNGER BROTHER OF LUDWIG, ACHIEVED ONLY FLEETING RECOGNITION WITH HIS EXPERIMENTAL COMPOSITION, "SONATA FOR PSYCHOPATHY."

Executing the Advisement Schmooze

Merlin goal: To sensitively acquire skills, knowledge, and wisdom by apprenticing yourself to a master adviser, or to make ordinary advisers advise you in a "master" way if they don't know how, have forgotten, or have grown indifferent.

- Again, you will need your sense of humor, but the situation outside the classroom is somewhat less formal. More whimsy, more sociability, and a more relaxed atmosphere are appropriate.

- Choose your own adviser. If assigned to one as a freshman, you are not condemned to that adviser for the duration. After some experience—and after you've asked upper-level students "Who's good?"—select another adviser, preferably in your major area.

- Make an appointment with the person you have selected and announce forthrightly that you have chosen him or her as your adviser if he or she would be willing to work with you. This simple act is so powerful. Even the most burned-out prof will sense that he or she is somehow special in your view.

- Be certain that the person you chose in this way really *is* special. Reputation around school, other students' shared experiences, and your own needs have somehow to enter into the choice. For these reasons, it is always a good idea, as mentioned, to select an adviser in your major area. After all, this person is pursuing a professional career that you hope to emulate or at least model yourself on some aspect of. An adviser in your major area and you are likely to talk the same language.

- Good advisers make appointment times to see their advisees, and they live by those times. Don't cancel appointments and never be a no-show. Behavior such as this will alienate your adviser and ruin what could be a productive relationship. *Common courtesy is the one thing that communicates respect for the other person in a relationship.* If your adviser is rude, he or she should be ashamed, but there is little you can do about another's rudeness. When a student is rude, the rudeness assures trouble for the student. Sounds unfair? It is unfair, but no one said that justice prevails in human relationships.

Be a Merlin; don't naively expect justice in relationships where one of the participants has more authority or power than the other.

- If you've chosen wisely, your adviser can teach you more than how to fill out your schedule for the semester. In psychology, for example, your adviser can tell you about the various specialties that professionals practice from a more real vantage point than texts or graduate catalogs can. Your adviser can tell you how to plan your undergraduate course work to prepare yourself for the competition involved in applying to graduate and professional schools, or for the real-world applications of your undergraduate major. The essential ingredient: *You* must ask.

- In many departments, a student's major adviser is also the mentor for the senior project. Sometimes the adviser is a supervisor for fieldwork internships and will guide the writing of your research report. It is therefore very important to work closely and well with the adviser, because you have the opportunity under these conditions for an exciting experience: learning by apprenticeship. To my way of thinking, some lessons can be learned only in a one-to-one teaching relationship. Good writing and editing skills can be acquired in this way. A sense of how to organize data and critically interpret them can be learned by watching an experienced organizer and interpreter operate. These are the valuable out-of-the-classroom learning experiences that good advisement includes. Again, you get only what you ask for.

Here is an example of a *good* advisement schmooze:

"Professor Melancholy, I've researched the topic in the library, and I've gotten copies of about twenty-five journal articles. But I'm having a hard time putting them together. I can't find a common thread. Is there a way to do this? Can you tell me where to look to see how it's done?"

Contrast the good schmooze with this *poor* advisement schmooze:

"Professor Panarrogance, I can't find anything much on the topic. Here's what I've got so far. It doesn't really go together. What else should I look up? Can you look at this stuff and tell me how it goes together?"

The difference between the good and the poor schmoozes is clear. A good schmooze is likely to elicit from the prof usable help in the form of suggestions and demonstrations of how to read the material for a common theme. This appropriately schmoozed adviser will want to help, because the student is asking for a personal demonstration, not for the prof to make it easier or to do the work.

In the poor schmooze, the student begins with a complaint of futility. The schmooze is more likely to annoy than to elicit helpful advising. In this second example, the student has not demonstrated effective personal effort on which to base further requests for help. An arrogant adviser will experience the request as a whiny complaint, a narcissistic professor will interpret it as a personal criticism that he or she has not done enough for you, and an indifferent adviser will be prompted to dismiss you with a curt "go back to the drawing board" kind of reply (for your own good, of course).

About Merlin Advisers

At most colleges the question "Who should advise?" is the subject of great debate. Not every teacher is a good adviser. As a rule of thumb, the qualities of the Merlin professor discussed in Chapter 2 are the qualities of the Merlin adviser. It might be helpful to go back and review them.

The Merlin adviser has additional features, however, that you'll recognize as you make your choice. Remember that you have, usually, more flexibility in choosing an adviser than in choosing teachers, because there are generally more advisers available than teachers who give specific courses you need or want. Also remember, a poor first or second choice is not fatal. With appropriate assertiveness, you are free to switch advisers. Here are some observable characteristics of Merlin advisers to help you make a satisfying choice the first time:

- Merlin advisers do not present themselves as frantic, harassed people who barely make time for advisement interviews. They are calm, welcoming people who appear to enjoy the one-to-one contact with students, and view such contacts as opportunities for powerful learning.

- Merlin advisers are approachable in an appropriately friendly way. They do not stand on ceremony; that is, they are professional but relaxed in their one-to-one dealings with advisees. They will share personal experiences that are instructive, they evidence a real concern for your welfare as you mature through your college experiences, and they know where to draw the line to prevent intrusion into your personal life.

- Merlin advisers, like Merlin profs, know their stuff. They are knowledgeable about not only the subject matter they teach, but also the requirements for success and satisfaction in the academic field they represent. And they are eager to share this nonclassroom knowledge with you. When you ask them, a light goes on in their eyes, they sit forward in their chairs, and their voices take on an excited quality as they talk to you about what it's like to be a management consultant, or a computer artificial intelligence expert, or a psychologist, or an engineer, or an artist, or a dancer, or a musician, or a historian, or a philosopher. (What does a good metaphysician make a week now?)

- Merlin advisers do not hesitate to advise, even when that advice is a warning of impending academic disaster, even when that advice is an admonition to get your act together or else, and even when that advice is the last thing you want to hear. Such advisement is difficult to do, and all academic advisers agree that such work with students has an emotional price. But the Merlin adviser is able to be the person who gives you a needed kick in the behind without humiliating and without angering you, because the truth of the advice is plainly, if painfully, evident to both of you.

Some Summary, Some Conclusions

☆ The Merlin appropriately sensitive schmooze is a technique for actively participating in your own education with teachers or advisers who have grown distracted, weary, or uncaring.

☆ The skillful Merlin schmooze structures the learning situation so that a teacher or adviser is prompted to give his or her best efforts, but it takes planning and effort on the student's part as well.

☆ The good schmooze requires:

1. gentle encouragement of humor

2. thoughtful preparation of questions with structure and content

3. an implied invitation for the prof to share the expertise you admire.

☆ Skillful schmooze execution requires great personal control over anger and urges to sarcasm.

Each day Merlin tried to be kind to people, but it made his teeth hurt.

About This Chapter

Main Theme of the Chapter
Both students and teachers have unrealistic expectations about tests. The simple truth is that tests are a timely and reasonable command to study. Everything else you might have heard about classroom testing is pure myth, including take-home tests, or tests designed to flunk half a class, or tests that have nothing to do with what you were taught.

Related Ideas

☆ Test realities

☆ Test preparation divided into before, during, and after

☆ Controlling text anxiety

☆ How to write answers in Merlin's special format designed to please teachers and organize your writing

CHAPTER 5

How to Take Tests

Classroom tests can be fruitful stimuli to learning, or they can be laxatives for the mind. Few people like tests. Profs find them a burden to prepare and to grade. Students are made anxious and angry by them. Yet the educational system has its own momentum. Throughout your college career, you will spend between 25 and 40 percent of your time preparing for and taking examinations. Tests will range from straightforward assessments of remembered course content to measurements that attempt to predict how well you will do in graduate school.

You will be exposed to all manner of test myth and realities such as:

- the paradoxical *take-home test*

- the intimidating *weekly quiz*

- the excruciating *comprehensive midterm exam*

- and even the ultimate educational assault on the beachhead of student resistance to knowledge: *the cumulative final exam.*

Welcome to education.

By graduation, you will no doubt be committed to the traditional test enterprise. If asked whether you would like to see future students freed from examinations, you will feel compelled to answer: "No. I would not!" The reasons for your answer will be mixed: You will have learned the hard way that tests are an indispensable part of the college learning process, and you will convince yourself that new students should face the same struggles you faced. Merlin cannot do much to alter the misery-loves-company motive, but there is no need for you to learn the value of tests the hard way. You can learn how to take tests with less wear and tear on your emotional well-being, and with more productive demonstrations of how much you have learned.

Fact and Folklore of Tests: What You Need to Know

A Merlin prof's chief aim in making and giving tests is to assure that students actually read and study the assigned course materials. That means, simply, the prof knows it is easy to sit in class taking voluminous notes and to read a text like a novel once in a while, but that actually absorbing information, concepts, and ideas requires prolonged, effort-ful, active *study*. Tests provide periodic commands to study that even the most self-motivated student needs in order to proceed consistently and efficiently.

A secondary motive, of course, is that test performance is the way to monitor and evaluate student learning or the lack of it. The theory is that each student in the class is exposed to the same set of class experiences, has access to the same study materials, and demonstrates an individual level of learning by performance on a uniform examination. Grades can be assigned on the basis of comparing students' test answers, and by comparing the class performance against a quality standard set by the individual prof. That's the theory.

Test grades and careful test-paper comments by the professor also serve as feedback to students so that they know how successful their learning efforts are and whether to accelerate or continue what they are doing.

In plainer terms, tests are given to:

1. Enforce study of the course content: a timely command to study.

2 Evaluate the level and quality of individual learning.

3. Provide feedback to the student to improve or maintain achievement.

If you look at this list, you have the reasons profs make and give tests. These ideas are what they're thinking about throughout this enterprise. Knowing these ideas gives you a powerful advantage, as will be clear shortly. The important point, although you will not believe it right now, is that this list *really* is all there is to college tests. Really. Everything else you may have heard falls into the realm of test mythology (or sometimes into the domain of test felonies perpetrated by inept teachers).

Test Mythology

Here are some ideas that either have no foundation in the reality of the teaching-learning-testing enterprise or that embody distortions introduced into the enterprise by ill-informed teachers.

- *Tests have to be as difficult as possible and demand only superior-level performance from students, so that as many students fail as pass.*

Reality: A sound, well-constructed classroom test asks for information, ideas, or skills that were taught. Making the test questions tricky, more difficult than, or only remotely related to what was taught defeats the purpose of the test, cheats the student, and distorts the meaning of "education." Only a sadistic teacher would construct tests in this way, and if the teacher is that sadistic, tests are the least of your worries. Moreover, most teachers would not care if on a fair test the whole class earned passing, even superior, grades. In fact, I might throw a party.

HARE-BRAINED IDEA Ⅳ:
"MOHAWK"

- *Comprehensive final examinations are a "real" test of what students have learned, and anything less than this is watering down the quality of the student's education.*

Reality: Comprehensive exams can be a productive teaching-learning tool, but not a necessary one. If a comprehensive final exam is the only test for the course, it has undue academic and emotional weight. One disadvantage is that "big finals" covering the whole course force massive memorizing that results in a very well-informed student on examination day. One week later, however, the depth of the information is lost; within two weeks, details are fuzzy, and by the end of the following semester, substance and organization have vanished for all but the most exceptional human beings.

- *A clever way to test is to "surprise" students with such questions as "Write all you have learned about this course in the next three hours" or "Pick the idea you value most in this course, and explain it completely."*

Reality: Except, perhaps, at the highest levels of the educational enterprise, say postdoctoral study, such "testing" is more a challenge to the student's frustration tolerance than to intellectual achievement. A test felony such as this is perpetrated by profs who pride themselves on their cleverness and intellectual expertise. They are making academic asses of themselves. Tests such as the ones described above might permit the very, very bright student to display some brilliance, but they will not promote continued learning, provide regular feedback, or serve in any way as a reasonable command to study.

- *A take-home test can stand in lieu of a classroom examination or as a makeup for a classroom exam that was a disaster.*

Reality: At best, the take-home examination is a misuse of the term *test.* At worst, students are led to believe that the take-home test is equivalent to periodic classroom evaluations. In fact, such "tests" are really term projects or term paper assignments that require research, or outside reading, or use of course readings; such "tests" do not accomplish the same thing as classroom exams. They do not

serve as a command to study. Take-homes serve as a command to
organize, or problem-solve, or write lengthy, copied answers from
sources. A take-home "test" can be a legitimate educational procedure, but it should not substitute for timely classroom tests nor
should it be presented to students as other than what it is: namely,
a homework assignment.

- *A test on which it is impossible for students to determine how much
weight is assigned to each question is valuable: It keeps 'em guessing.*

Reality: If you don't know how much each question is worth, you
can't ration the amount of time and effort you will devote to each
item or essay. You may very well lavish attention and precious test
time on a 10-point item, while breezing through a 25-point item
because the 10-pointer "looks" more difficult. Or
perhaps all the items are the same credit value:
Then it pays not to spend a disproportionate
amount of time on items you find difficult.
They're all worth the same. Merlin profs
know and plan for these contingencies.
They construct well-balanced tests that
provide good feedback to the student.
Taking a test is not an adventure, nor is
it a detective mystery. It is merely a test.

THE
HALF-ASSESSED
SCHOLAR

M

Dear Test Taker:

Did you know that the word *examination* comes from the Latin *examinare*, "to weigh accurately"? Scholar's battle cry: "Get weighed!"

Etymologically yours,

Merlin

What You Know About Tests

Tests should be:

- reasonable and timely commands to study

- measures of what you have been taught

- fair and balanced: not super-hard nor super-easy

- given as classroom exams, not as homework assignments.

Taking Tests the Merlin Way

Like so many things in life, test taking has three parts: before, during, and after.

Before is the night before the exam, when Merlin preparation can help reduce test anxiety and make intense study effective.

During is the actual writing of the test answers following Merlin techniques that maximize the readability of your responses and enhance their quality in the eyes of the examiner.

After is the day the graded tests are returned to you, when Merlin principles can guide your "recovery" for the next exam, or help you to maintain the high level of achievement you earned.

The Merlin Art of Test Preparation

Despite what you may have heard to the contrary, cramming the night before, if done correctly, is one of the most effective ways of preparing for an exam. The term *cramming* has an unsavory connotation among teachers, but, in fact, what cramming usually means is an effortful study session designed to stuff a lot of facts and concepts into your head right before you need them. Merlin gives his blessings.

The surest way to pass a test is to study completely and comprehensively and exhaustively for it. As they say in the oatmeal commercials, "It's the right thing to do." But that kind of study is most productive when it builds on prior periods of preparation: reading the assigned work continuously, completing lab and homework assignments regularly, attending lectures religiously. In other words, you must think of cramming as a climax to a long prelude of reliable work rather than as a last-minute way to save your behind.

CHAPTER FIVE

It's impossible to cram effectively the night before a test if you have not prepared the materials and yourself adequately. A textbook chapter of twenty-five to thirty pages that has not been read, underlined, and understood prior to study cannot be crammed. A half notebook of lecture notes largely copied from classmates because you were absent from class most of the time will not yield much that is useful for a cramming session. And any kind of a practical examination, such as a biology or chemistry lab practicum, will be a nightmare if you are not conversant with the techniques and materials from many previous hours of steady work.

A cram is a "good" cram only if what you're stuffing into your head is already familiar and organized. Here's how to do it effectively:

- Familiarize yourself with the bulk of the material that has been assigned for the test. Look it over in its entirety to get a sense of how much there is, how long learning it will take, and how difficult the material is for you. If you've been working steadily throughout the course, this step is actually already completed by the time a first test rolls around.

- If there is more than one source of information for the test, make a list of the order in which you will study the material—for example, lecture notes, textbook chapters, outside readings, reserve materials from the library. As a general rule of thumb (but with exceptions when you have a nonteaching teacher for the course), it is almost always best to start with lecture notes. These notes represent the ideas and organization regarded as important by the teacher—that is, by the person who will make up the test. So you can, by studying the lecture material first, develop a mental road map of the whole territory to be covered, especially what to emphasize and what to ignore.

- Study your text materials according to the *Survey 3RQ* method discussed in Chapter 6. **S**urvey the whole, **r**ead it, **r**ecite it, **r**eview it, and then **q**uestion yourself on it.

By the time you're done with the text or readings, you ought to be able to generate questions that you would ask students if you were teaching them that material. More often than not, you will ask questions of yourself the night before the test that are virtually identical to the ones that will actually be asked by the prof.

- The key point in this preparation sequence is to be active. Passive reading of text or lecture material is *not* studying. I would prefer actually to see a student cram hard three or four times in a college semester than passively read through texts and notes routinely each week with the false belief that such "reading" is equivalent to learning the course material. Be active. Exert effort.

You *should* feel tired from this enterprise. And, if you have done it well, you will feel satisfied when you see your grades and sense the growth in your knowledge.

(*Merlin hint:* If you want to see how much you have really learned from all this effort, imagine trying to teach some students who are just beginning to study the subject you've learned about. Think about how much *they* don't yet know, and how what you now take for granted, they have yet to understand.)

The Merlin Art of Test Taking

Preparation is 95 percent of test success. However, you can increase your efficiency with some modest behavioral techniques during the writing of the test answers. None of the following suggestions is powerful enough to rescue a test taker who has not prepared adequately. Nor will any of these performance aids elevate a failing grade to a passing one. But they will give you the extra edge to turn a B into a B+ or a C into a C+.

Combined with the slightly more powerful techniques to manage test anxiety discussed later in the chapter, these humble test-writing strategies can make test taking, if not pleasant, at least manageable. Each of them is designed to give you more control over the test situation itself. Here are some workable strategies in the Merlin art of test taking:

- If the test will be a lengthy one (more than ninety minutes), take a candy bar with you to supplement your physical energy for the long haul. About one hour into the exam, eat it. Even if the "sugar hit" does not boost your flagging energy, at least it's something to look forward to.

- If you're tense, chew gum throughout the test. It's better than pencil tapping, which makes everyone want to kill you.

- Always start with the question you know the most about, and answer it fully. Even if this question is not the first in the test, it does not matter. By answering the one you know or like best, you build confidence, you give yourself time to assimilate the rest of the exam, and you do not permit yourself to grow more anxious while you puzzle over items that are more difficult or that you do not recognize. Begin with what you know.

Multiple-Choice Tests

- **Eliminate, don't guess wildly.** Understand that multiple-choice items require you to *recognize* rather than produce the correct answer. For that reason, think of this kind of test as a discrimination task in which you have to find the target among the distractors. Of course, the better you know the correct answer, the easier finding it becomes. But if you eliminate as many of the misleading distractors as you can, your odds of selecting the target choice are higher. Thus if you can eliminate at least two of the four choices on logical grounds alone, your task is to select only one out of two possible answers for that question. Eliminate, and be ruthless.

- **Don't second-guess yourself.** Some evidence in the psychology of signal detection theory shows that your first impulse is usually correct when picking a target answer in the multiple-choice format. In other words, don't agonize. Don't continually return to items and change them for what now looks like a better answer. Multiple-choice items are usually not that profound, so the item you selected by eliminating the wrong items the first time is more likely to be correct than your second-time-around choice.

- **Don't agonize over one impossible item.** Never spend a disproportionate amount of your time on one or two items that are difficult. They are usually all worth the same amount of credit, so go on to those you can answer. If you have time later, return to the difficult, unanswered ones and complete them. Best strategy is always to get as many right as you can, not merely answer them all at the cost of rushing through the ones you could have gotten right if you had not lost so much time on the "impossible" ones. This technique is very helpful on mathematics, statistics, chemistry, and physics tests, where numerical calculation problems dominate.

- **Avoid humorous or illogical choices.** Many question writers include one or more questions that have ridiculous, often funny, choices to relieve the tension of test taking. It is generally true that the funny or absurdly illogical item is *rarely* the correct one. Enjoy such questions, but don't be tempted. Advantage: A humorous choice automatically narrows your selection to three in a four-choice question.

- **Be a question detective.** Use the information contained in the questions from all parts of the test to help you discriminate the correct choice on particular questions. The stems (the question part of a multiple-choice item) frequently contain additional information about other items in the test.

Practice Question:
From which major psychological disorder
   does the person pictured here suffer?

a. terminal testitis
b. premature examination
c. displaced GRE
d. cheating interruptus
e. death

- **"All of these"** and **"none of these"** are generally included in multiple-choice questions when the test writer runs out of plausible alternatives. A sound item using one of these as the correct answer is very difficult to write. Consider selecting this answer only when test directions specify it as the task, or when you know it to be correct. *When in doubt,* the odds are with you if you consider "all" or "none" as distractors and eliminate them. ("In doubt" means that you don't have a clue to the right answer. Then, and only then, the odds are with you in eliminating "all of these" and "none of these" from your considerations.)

- **True-or-false** items are not used much, but there is a quirky thing about such questions you should know. It is far easier to write a "true" stem than to write a plausible false one. So when in doubt, and you have no other clue to whether an item is true or false, and you have to guess anyway, then guess "true." The odds are with you.

Essay Tests

Unlike multiple-choice, fill-in, or true-false questions, essay exams demand full recall rather than mere recognition. Essays place a premium on good writing skills, good organization skills, and your ability to answer with precision and speed. In short, you really have to know your stuff.

Essays place a premium on the professor's effort and time as well. In general, essay exams are not much used in sections of courses that have 100 or more students in them. The reason is simple: No professor could read and grade that many essay exams. For example, if there are 100 students in a course, and a test consists of 3 essays, the professor has to read 300 essays. These 300 essays translate to something on the order of 300 to 800 pages of writing! And that assumes only one exam in the semester for this one course. Because professors' work loads usually include three or four courses per semester, each with its own tests, quizzes, and term papers, plus whatever number of advisees and senior theses that semester brings, it is unlikely that you will get essay exams in large lecture courses.

Know, therefore, that when a professor assigns essay exams, he or she takes them seriously, will probably read them thoroughly, and expects more than mere "shovel swinging" from you. Essays are hard to grade and harder still for professors to look forward to when their students don't take them seriously or prepare for them productively. Assigning low grades to poor essays or to irritating writing and organizational habits is easy when you have to read 300 to 500 pages of material! Take the hint.

Here are some tips to increase your efficiency and help you get the most out of "halo effects" that can enhance your essays. Remember, part of writing an effective answer to an essay is to please your audience: namely, the teacher who asked the question. But if you don't really have the facts and concepts in your head, these hints won't help much.

Essay answers should be narrations that tell the "story" of your thinking and learning on the subject of the questions. Like any good narrative, the essay answer should have a clear beginning, middle, and end that your reader can easily identify. In fact, good essay answers should follow the age-old formula for good communication of any kind (preview, content, and summary):

1. Tell them what you're going to tell them.

2. Tell them.

3. Tell them what you told them.

1. Tell them what you're going to tell them. A statement, usually in one sentence or two, of the territory you will cover in your answer. Such a statement should incorporate the main features of the question you were asked. For example:

Question: Evaluate the term *abnormal* as it is used in contemporary psychopathology, and include in your essay the various ways this concept has been defined and the reasons it is a controversial label.

CHAPTER FIVE

Opening sentence: "The term *abnormal* has had at least three different historical meanings in psychology that ranged from purely statistical definitions to medical definitions to definitions based on a person's feelings of distress. For reasons that I will discuss, each definition of *abnormal* emphasized only one aspect of disordered behavior while ignoring other important features."

 M

Merlin's Recipe for Essays

- Tell 'em what you're going to tell 'em.

- TELL 'em.

- Tell 'em what you told 'em.

It is worth pointing out that this recipe for writing essays is a very good strategy for any kind of writing, and even for "public speaking" presentations.

2. Tell them. After the opening sentence or two, you write the body of your essay, which elaborates the plan you stated in the opening. This part of your essay is a narrative that actually answers the question asked. It should be detailed, factual, integrated, and follow the organization you announced in the first sentence. You can take a quick minute to jot on the back of the test paper ideas that you want to cover. You can even use arrows or a numbering system to organize your ideas so that they flow in a coherent way. But think of the body or narrative part of your essay as a story that has to be logical, consistent, and relevant.

How to tell them?

- *Use several paragraphs,* each with an opening sentence that states the main idea of that paragraph. And each such main idea should be one that you indicated you would talk about.

- *Underline important ideas* to guide your reader (who will probably be reading many exam papers and will be grateful for any organizational and reading aids).

- *Sprinkle with concrete examples* wherever relevant, giving credit to your text or class discussions where necessary. Show what you have learned in every way possible.

- *Write clearly, legibly, and calmly.* A paper that has to be decoded or in which the reader has to find marginal notes or insertions from other pages or make sense of chaotic handwriting annoys and fatigues the reader. Major hints: Don't fatigue the reader. Don't annoy the reader. Don't frustrate the reader. Do everything to make the reading pleasurable and speedy.

- *Mix your sentence structure.* On the whole, keep your sentences brief. Opening sentences for a paragraph in an essay answer are more effective if short and of declarative form. Intersperse some more complex sentences, or longer ones if the ideas to be expressed require them. But remember, on an exam your goal is to show what you know and how much you know to a reader who is evaluating everyone else's attempts to show the same things. Be memorable by being lucidly clear and precisely concise.

- *Pace yourself* to give the most detail in the questions worth the most credit. All your essays in a given examination should follow this format, but time limitations have to govern where you will put your maximum effort. There is not much use writing one elegantly constructed essay and three rushed or incomplete ones in a test that requires you to answer three or four questions in the time allotted. What you gain in credit for the good essay, you will more than lose in the poorly written ones.

3. Tell them what you told them. Your last job in writing an effective essay is to summarize *briefly* the main points you wrote about in the body of your essay. Don't take time to prepare a major summary. A simple one will do. You start a new and final paragraph with a phrase such as "In summary . . ." *or* "The key conclusions we have drawn from . . ." *or* "It is probably worthwhile to point out that . . ."

The purpose of the brief summary statement is to remind your reader of the key elements of the answer he or she has just read, and to tie up loose ends. It is a wise idea to underline any key words that appear in your summary, such as the names of concepts or people you discussed.

The Good, the Bad, and the Ugly

In the next few pages three different answers to an essay-test question given in an introductory psychology course are reproduced. One of the answers is a very competent response written under test time pressures, whereas the second essay is quite poor for all the reasons indicated, and the third answer is downright ugly. The good essay would receive the equivalent of a B, the poorer response a D, and the poorest an F.

The Good Essay

Question: What makes a reinforcer reinforcing?

Answer: In response to the question of what makes a reinforcer reinforcing, the truth is that we really are not sure. Effective reinforcement has been shown to result from <u>drive reduction</u>, <u>drive arousal</u> and from <u>arranging priorities</u> of preferred activities. Skinner himself simply limited the definition to a description of what increases or decreases the probability of response being made.

<u>Skinner's Law of Effect</u> (Empirical):

1. Anything that increases the probability of the occurrence of a certain response is called a <u>positive reinforcer</u>. For example, putting money in a slot machine and then winning increases the likelihood of you putting more money in. The prize money is the reinforcer.

2. Anything that decreases the probability of a response occurring is called a negative reinforcer. *[Note: This is a factual error.]* Getting bad grades on an exam will decrease the probability that you will party again the night before your next exam. The bad grades are a negative reinforcer. *[Actually, this is a somewhat confused example of "punishment," not of negative reinforcement.]*

3. Anything that suppresses or prevents a response from occurring is a <u>punishment.</u>
[Note: Continuation of the error, but it is not completely erroneous.] Smaking [*sic*] a child's hand when he runs out into the street is preventing the child from running into the street again. *[Actually, this example is correct, but explained in the wrong terms.]* The smack on the hand is the punishment.

Sheffield, Baecker & Wolff studied the behavior of rats in a T-maze. A female animal in estrous [*sic*] was in one corner of the maze and a male animal (inexperienced sexually) was in the start box. They watched the animal run to the female and attempt to mount her and took the male away before orgasm was achieved. This was repeated a large number of times, and the males never stopped running to the female even though they were never satisfied. There was no drive reduction, yet the males continued to solve the maze problem for drive arousal. So drive reduction is obviously not the ingredient in reinforcing these animals.

Premack Principle: Premack said that any less desirable behavior can be performed or increased when it is rewarded by a more favorable behavior. For example, a child who prefers watching TV to playing a pool table game, can be told he can watch TV only after he has played pool for 15 minutes. TV is the reinforcer increasing pool-playing. Later, it can be reversed, and he will be allowed to play pool only if he watches 15 minutes of TV.

Summary: Skinner was probably right, as pointed out in class, to limit his definition of reinforcement to just a statement of probabilities. What makes a reinforcer reinforcing is very variable, and probably depends, for human beings, on additional factors like what a situation means to them. It is not possible to limit the definition to drive reduction because so many reinforcers do not reduce drives. It is also not possible to limit the definition to drive inducers (arousers) for the same reason of many exceptions. However, the Premack Principle, like Skinner's own definition, is descriptive rather than "prescriptive." It specifies a functional probability relationship based on direct observation.

Grade: B

Notice that the good essay reads easily. Although we can't reproduce handwriting here, it was written neatly and legibly. The spelling, grammar, punctuation, and underlining of the original have been retained. Observe the opening sentence and how it directly tells the reader what territory will be covered, and note that precisely that territory is discussed in the body of the essay.

By the time you get through the narrative section, you have a clear idea of how much this student knows about the subject matter, and how she brings it to bear *on the question asked.* The student writer emphasizes her three main points with underlining and examples. Note also that the body of the essay is organized to parallel the statement given at the beginning, and that a concise but helpful reminder summary appears at the end.

Be aware that although the writing in this essay is far from qualifying as literature, it is sound, correct, clear English prose. The organization is competent and logical. Examples are called "examples," and evidence from reading and class discussion is referred to in an identifiable way.

When I read and graded this essay, I had three things in mind that shaped the B grade I gave it. I'm guessing that most teachers would have similar ideas as they read an answer such as this one. Here are the reasons this essay earned a B rather than a B+ or an A.

- The essay lacks transitions between ideas. Some factual details are wrong.

- The essay writer makes an attempt to communicate clearly the three main areas she will cover, and summarizes a key conclusion (actually an inference based on class discussions) that is directly relevant to the question.To earn a B+ or an A, I would have expected no factual errors, an attempt to integrate the three main ideas into a relevant statement about reinforcement in general, and additional facts and concepts from the textbook readings (such as the biological basis of reinforcement in the hypothalamus).

The Bad Essay

Question: *What makes a reinforcer reinforcing?*

Answer: There are different kinds of reinforcers. There are positive, negative, primary, and secondary. Each in some way strengthens a response. A (1) positive reinforcer is a reward given when the subject performs how he is supposed to. In this case, he will repeat the performance if continually reinforced *[Note: So far, this response is confused, irrelevant to the question, and factually wrong.]* There are negative (2) reinforcers. These also strengthen responses. Negative reinforcers are like warnings, a shock for instance, on the floor of a rats cage in order that the rat push a lever, his floor is shocked less each time he pushes the lever. Therefore, he continually will push the lever if shocks are withheld. There are (3) primary reinforcers, such as food in order to stop hunger, and (4) secondary reinforcers, such as money for humans. Money is a means for primary reinforcers.

Work: Skinner's Empirical Law of Effect stated that positive reinforcers would condition the subject, because of the pleasure. Negative reinforcers would condition the subject, they avoid pain, and that they will do anything to avoid punishment. Skinner experimented with laboratory rats in cages (shock method) in order to prove his theory. *[Note: It is very clear by now from the poor writing, poor logic, and continued factual errors that this student does not know nor can she express the concepts for which the question asked. She's in the right city, but has yet to even find the ballpark.]*

The Premack Principle states that if there are two positive reinforcers and one is more desirable than the other, if the less desirable one is distributed, and the more desirable one follows, the subject will go through the less desirable to reach the more desirable. For instance, if a child has to do his homework in order to watch TV, the homework will be done in order to be able to watch TV. The TV works as an incentive.

Grade: D

It is painful to read an essay such as this one. When I graded it, I was feeling very generous and had these ideas in mind:

- It is still an introductory psychology course and I should expect only an elementary level of understanding.

- The essay is not an answer to the question asked, but rather a rambling, poorly written collection of largely erroneous ideas about reinforcement in general.

- The poor writing reflects poor study and poor thinking.

- There are some factually correct ideas here, and the last paragraph of the essay is relevant to the question. Partial credit applies, but just barely.

- The writer has made no attempt to organize, synthesize, or express her ideas clearly to the reader. I must assume that the ideas are not clear for her, and I suspect that very little study has occurred.

- I graded the essay D, but some teachers would easily justify a grade of F.

The Ugly Essay

Question: *What makes a reinforcer reinforcing?*

Answer: What makes a reinforcer reinforcing? There is no answer to that question. Skinner's law of effect states that anything that rewards a response is a positive reinforcer. *[Note: Factual error.]* Premack's principle states that two behaviors differ in their likelihood of occurrence. *[Note: Conceptual error. No substance at all here.]* <u>Example</u>: All children love candy, but they don't like to clean their rooms. If they clean their room, they will be rewarded with a piece of candy. Reinforcement is still a mystery in psychology.

Grade: F

Trees should not be killed to make the paper to permit such ugliness to be transcribed. Why? Because:

- It is factually, conceptually, and logically wrong. Such deliberate ignorance is a waste of good tuition money.

- The "essay" completely lacks detail or any attempt to demonstrate understanding of the subject matter. Whatever the student could remember from having attended a class or two was thrown down here without thought or preparation. It demonstrates an uncaring attitude—for the teacher, for the subject matter, but most of all, for the student himself or herself. This uncaring attitude is ugly. (By the way, don't confuse "ugliness" with brevity. Even with more words, this "essay" would remain ugly.)

The Art of Test Recovery

When you've finished your examination, there are still some things you can do to improve your performance. You may not be able to do much about the test you just took, but you can use the experience to make the next one a more positive experience. Here are some Merlin hints.

- If possible, take the question paper with you when leaving the test. Most teachers will let you do this. If not, jot down as many of the questions as you can remember, so that you can review them at home. In this way, you can preview what your grades are likely to be before the exam is returned graded. (Obviously, this strategy is not possible for a multiple-choice test.) As you check over the test at home, in a calm atmosphere, you will see the things you could have done had you been less tense. And you can begin to develop an ear for the teacher's style of questioning. Thus, recovery from *this* exam is preparation for the next.

- Above all else, do something nice for yourself. Treat yourself to something you like: good food, a great movie, good company, a good sleep. Do whatever will make you release the tension of the exam and feel relaxed. Teachers usually cannot reward effort by itself, but *you* can. Reward the effort you have made. You deserve it, regardless of the grade you eventually receive.

- When you get your graded paper some days after the exam, don't just look at the grade. Spend some time reading the teacher's comments and try to learn from them how to write the next test. There's always a "next" test.

- Last, remember *Merlin's Rule:* Exams are "timely and reasonable commands to study." They are not a reflection of your ultimate worth as a human being. Mazel tov.

Test Anxiety

Mark Twain once said that he had read so much about the dangers of smoking, he decided to give up reading. If reading about test anxiety will make you anxious, don't read this section. There is no psychological condition more contagious than anxiety, so if you don't have this problem (and you'd be the one to know), don't try to fix it.

Everyone becomes anxious taking tests. A test, after all, is an evaluation. But an evaluation of what? Of you? Of your worth? Of your innate capacities? Not bloody likely. Even the best designed psychometric instruments fall far short of measuring such qualities. And no classroom test that I have seen could do it either. Almost always, a classroom test is an assessment of how much you have studied and how reliably you have attended classes in which you participated. Period.

Of course, a classroom test is still a *test*. You ought to be a little anxious. From the early 1900s it has been known that a small amount of anxiety is not only normal, it is helpful on intellectual tasks. In 1908 Yerkes and Dodson first demonstrated an elementary form of this truism. More recent research shows that a small amount of anxiety is helpful on very complex tasks, slightly larger amounts are tolerable on moderately complex tasks, and substantial amounts of anxiety do not affect performance on very, very simple tasks.

In short, amounts of anxiety can vary from helpful to disorganizing, depending on the task and on the person's experience with the task. What might be moderate anxiety for one person could very well be disorganizing stress for another. The key problem for the test-anxious person is not the anxiety itself, but the meaning the person ascribes to the distress he or she feels.

This meaning can elevate anxiety to the point that the person panics and cannot read the test items, or "blocks" and cannot remember anything from hours of study. I have seen test anxiety reduce a person to tears.

The Test-Anxious Person

Current research into the variables that contribute to test anxiety has led to some very confusing and contradictory findings. But one theme stands out: The meaning that the disabled test-anxious person places on the test is that test performance directly demonstrates his or her intellectual inferiority compared to other people.

Put another way, the nonanxious person is able to focus on the test questions, *but the test-anxious person focuses on self.* His or her thoughts are centered on negative self-images and negative anticipations of what others will think of him or her. Some researchers believe that this style reflects not only situational test anxiety but a long-term, learned personal style acquired through a history of failures, near failures, or humiliations.

To give you some more detailed idea of the variables that have been found to be associated with test anxiety, Figure 5.1 is a checklist of test-anxiety feelings and actions. You might want to treat the checklist like a self-diagnostic quiz, ignoring the irony of assessing test anxiety by taking a quiz. Following the figure is a more abstract list of findings on the test-anxious person to help you understand the factors that might be changed to reduce the distress.

CHAPTER FIVE

Are you test anxious?

Here are some psychological features of the test-anxious person drawn from the research literature and from the *Sarason Test Anxiety Questionnaire*. The items are phrased as questions that you might use to decide whether to seek assistance.

Do you . . .

1. Think about how much brighter the other students are than yourself when you are taking a test?

2. Worry about the consequences of failing the test rather than doing well?

3. Get so nervous before an important test that your stomach is upset?

4. Freeze up on big tests such as midterms and final exams?

5. Almost always feel after taking a test that you could have done better?

6. Become so anxious that you forget what you really know?

Would you . . .

1. Be more tense if you knew that the test was an intelligence test rather than an achievement test?

2. Agree with this statement: "The harder I work at taking a test or studying for one, the more confused I get?"

3. Prefer writing a paper, no matter how long, to taking a test?

4. Feel more comfortable if you were allowed to take tests alone, without time limits?

Figure 5.1

Test-anxious people:

- **Are self-focused rather than task-focused.** They think about the feelings of distress elicited by the test situation and about how badly they are doing rather than about the test or about how to solve the problems before them.

- **Blame themselves for stupidity or for emotional weakness.** From their own subjective viewpoint, they feel inept, incompetent, and at fault for their own distress and the failures it produces. This is a vicious circle: the more blame they place on self, the more anxious they become, and the more anxious they become, the more likely they are to fail a test. It follows that repeated failures reinforce their feelings of worthlessness and trigger the cycle over and over.

- **Think of each test as a measure of their innate intelligence rather than as a classroom assessment of what they have learned.** A point made repeatedly throughout *Merlin* is that no test is a measure of a student's worth or goodness or competence. Even intelligence tests for the most part measure only a small fraction of what intelligence is. A classroom test reflects nothing more than how well you learned the class materials and how efficient you are in producing output that is acceptable to the evaluator.

- **During a test forget basic problem-solving or coping skills that they otherwise use daily.** They "forget" while under stress the usual strategies they would use in more calm times, namely:

1. Look at all alternatives to a question or problem.

2. Write down your thoughts from what you studied and organize them logically.

3. Don't get trapped and panicked by one or two difficult items and assume all is lost.

4. Forget about what is going on around you, such as what other people are doing, and concentrate on the problem.

5. Recognize momentary forgetting of facts or blocking for what it is: *momentary*.

- **Ruminate or continually rethink an answer, changing it over and over in their minds until they are doubtful of everything.** Especially on multiple-choice exams, rumination (literally "rechewing and redigesting your food like a cow") is self-defeating. And on essay exams this cognitive style is displayed by the test-anxious person, who cannot write more than one or two sentences without wondering whether to change them.

- **Engage in panicky "self-talk" that intensifies anxiety and predicts disastrous failure.** Test-anxious people talk "panic talk" to themselves. Usually it's called "thinking." But test-anxious people's thinking is in the form of a monologue to self about how hard the test is, how much more they should have studied, how everybody else is doing fine by comparison, how stupid they are by comparison with other students, how the test seems never to end, how much they wish they were out of the test room, out of the course, out of the school. If you think about it, this is actually a list of "shoulds": Test-anxious people are telling themselves how they *should* be better than they are, how they *should* be like other people, and how they *should* be stronger, smarter, more controlled. In reality, what they *should* do is stop "shoulding" and think about the *test*.

Controlling Test Anxiety

When to Seek Assistance

Test anxiety comes in all degrees of intensity, and most forms will evaporate by themselves as you become more experienced. Moreover, a small degree of test anxiety is helpful, because it arouses you to a fuller state of attention than if you were blasé or bored. But intense test anxiety can be disabling, ruining a college career and blocking further education. Here's Merlin's operational definition of test anxiety sufficiently strong to warrant professional assistance:

- when the person's anxiety in taking tests or anticipating tests is high enough to make the person withdraw from courses, *or*

- withdraw from school, *or*

- change or abandon a cherished life goal or career plan to avoid tests.

If any one of these criteria applies to you, professional assistance is indicated. There is no need for this level of destructive distress. The best way to get competent help is to apply at your school's counseling center, academic advising office, or department of psychology for a referral.

Most test-anxious people dread doing this because they believe it reveals the worst about them. If you feel that way, the next best step is to consult a single faculty person you trust or you sense is an understanding person. He or she will refer you to the appropriate sources.

Things You Can Do to Help Yourself
If you are not test-anxious to the degree just discussed, there are several self-help strategies that emerge directly from the discussion of the variables associated with this distress. You can probably figure them out for yourself from our previous discussion, but here is a list anyway:

- *Focus on the problem at hand* (the test), and stop yourself from thinking about how bad, how frightened, or how uncomfortable you feel. Use scrap paper or the back of the test to jot down whatever question-relevant ideas spring to mind. Don't edit ideas for quality at this stage. Any and all associations to the question are valuable.

  Work from this list of ideas as you answer specific questions. Organize as you write. Remember that tests are a finite experience. *They end.* Don't rush, but be aware that when your work is finished, so is the test.

- *Begin your test focus before the day of the actual test.* Specifically, the Merlin techniques of preparing for and taking tests are your best defense against test anxiety. There is no more effective cure for test anxiety than knowing your stuff so well that it flows automatically.

- *During the test, stop yourself from comparisons with the students around you.* Because tests are graded, it is natural, inevitable, to compare ourselves with our peers. But delay the comparison until after the test. It will always look like they're not having trouble because, unless they are very dramatic people, they do not display their feelings.

- *Never permit the first question in a test to throw you.* If the first one is difficult for you, or if you block at the sight of the first question, be assured that this effect of anxiety is customary for anxious people. Skip the first item and save it for later. By the end of the test period, you will not block any more. The worst self-sabotage you can enact is to anticipate having trouble with the first question and then make your own prophecy come true. Be aware that everyone who is test anxious has this same nightmare. Detour past it, and you will control it.

- *Know in your heart that test anxiety is not a disease,* it is not a mental disorder, it is not a reflection of your character flaws. It is a learned, self-defeating set of actions that can be changed.

- *Avoid panicky self-talk.* Don't think about "after the test": Think about now. Stop all thoughts that begin with "the other students." Stop all thoughts about any important people in your life—such as teachers, parents, boyfriends or girlfriends. Think only about what you are doing on each question.

- *Learn behavioral relaxation and deep breathing exercises,* which some research has shown to be effective in reducing the effects of test anxiety. These techniques are easily learned through audio-tapes widely available in large bookstores and from short-term consultations with clinical and counseling psychologists. There is even a videotape in preparation designed to teach these relaxation techniques (a Jane Fonda workout for the mind?).

- *Resolve to share your distress with someone you trust*—a congenial professor, a friend, another student. Talking about it with an understanding person leads to corrective actions and emotional support. It does not reveal the worst about you. If you don't believe this, come and argue with me.

It should be fairly clear that the art of test taking is a learnable Merlin skill. Never hesitate to ask your profs questions about their tests. Make use of what you learn from one test to enhance your performance on the next one. But bear in mind that educational testing serves a useful, if painful, function. It is a reasonable and timely command to study.

Some Summary, Some Conclusions

☆ Classroom tests are the subject of many myths and abuses, but they serve one real function. They are *timely and reasonable commands to study.*

☆ The good test does only these things: assesses what you have been taught, provides a realistic challenge relative to other students at your level, and provides feedback to you to modify or maintain your performance.

☆ Merlin test preparation involves three parts:

1. *Before:* preparation using the Survey 3RQ method to be discussed in Chapter 6 and active organizing of text and lecture materials in effortful study.

2. *During:* modest behavioral techniques to focus attention and relieve tension.

3. *After:* using the test results to prepare for the next one.

☆ Multiple-choice tests require recognition of the correct answer.

☆ The key to a good essay is preparation, effective, clear writing, and the "tell them what you're going to tell them, tell them, and then tell them what you told them" format.

☆ Test anxiety can be a disabling form of distress when it is intense. In less intense forms, it reduces performance on tests. Merlin techniques of coping are learnable strategies to focus on the test rather than on self, and to avoid panicky self-talk.

☆

"Anticipation!" was Merlin's motto. But he kept confusing it with "constipation."

About This Chapter

Main Theme of the Chapter

Reading a textbook is touching other minds. Textbooks demand a kind of relationship from their readers that is different from what novels and short stories demand. You should:

☆ *Survey* the whole chapter of a text, using its headlines and summaries before reading the chapter.

☆ *Read* the chapter with a pencil in hand to underline and make notes in the margins to shorten the chapter for later study.

☆ *Recite* the main ideas you can recall from each section aloud as a kind of rehearsal.

☆ *Review* the whole chapter by telling yourself the "story" of the main themes coherently tied together through your own effort.

☆ *Question* yourself by constructing those questions about the chapter you would ask students if you were teaching.

Related Ideas

An aside on taking lecture notes, and advice on writing papers and how to profit from them.

CHAPTER 6

How to Read a Textbook, and Why

Reading a textbook is like having an intimate relationship with someone. It is an act of faith in the good intentions of your partner. As you view page upon page of words and pictures, you are meeting ideas that sprang from the minds of other people. Their thoughts will touch yours.

An author is your partner in thought. For better or worse, this intimate relationship between your mind and the mind of the unseen writer will change you. If you reflect for a moment, you might agree that the most interesting thing about other people is their thoughts. A textbook is an opportunity not only to "see" the thoughts of others but to observe how they organize them, work with them, expand them, make mistakes with them—to see how human minds function.

The secret of the universe that Merlin knew so well was that thoughts are expressed in a special language: words and pictures. Learn to be at home with words and pictures, to assimilate others' words and pictures and to create and communicate your own, and you will literally read (and create) people's thoughts.

Textbooks are different from other kinds of books. They are less artful than novels or short stories. And they require of the reader a different kind of attention. Authors of textbooks place a premium on organization, compartmenting ideas into a hierarchy of word packages.

Such packages come in different sizes, ranging from chapters to sub-divisions of chapters to single-page illustrations and boxed summaries.

Reading a text is a lot like navigating a maze: The reader must look for landmarks, pause at obstacles, and follow the "map" the author provides through unknown terrain. Of all the signposts on the author's map to the reader, the most significant are called headings. Readers accustomed to reading novels, short stories, or written versions of drama sometimes do not understand how to use textbook road signs, including headings, effectively.

You will not be engaged by the "story" of a textbook chapter the way you are by the plot of a good novel. You will not be guided in your reading by the unity that is found in a well-constructed work of fiction. And you will not be supported emotionally or sustained intellectually by the author's skillful manipulation of suspense and sympathy for the characters. With a textbook in hand, *you* have to be the guide, *you* have to provide the coherence, and *you* have to persist. Here's how.

Survey 3RQ

Some years ago, a method of reading textbook and technical material was developed at Ohio State University (reported by Robinson 1961; see the "Where Merlin's Ideas Come From" section at the end of *Merlin*). Initially it was called the *Survey Q3R* technique, for "Survey, Question, Read, Recite, Review." With time, the method evolved and became the more elaborate *PQ4R* method of "Preview, Question, Read, Reflect, Recite, Review," with a different Robinson involved (Thomas and Robinson 1972).

Both the simpler and more elaborate methods share a common theme: The reader must actively organize the ideas appearing on the page. In what follows, a Merlin modification of the original Survey Q3R is presented in detail. The changes introduced here are desirable for their simplicity and directness.

To get started on the right track, consult the overview of *Merlin's* version, Survey 3RQ, in Figure 6.1. It will help give you a picture of the whole method before you examine all the steps in detail on the pages that follow.

Merlin's Version of **Survey 3RQ**

☆ SURVEY IT

- Scan whole chapter

- Read main heads

- Read chapter summary

☆ READ IT by underlining and using marginal notes.

☆ RECITE IT out loud by saying to yourself the ideas you can remember.

☆ REVIEW IT by closing the book and telling yourself the "story" of the chapter.

☆ Ask QUESTIONS of yourself that you would ask students if you were teaching the material.

Figure 6.1

The method involves five steps that focus your attention and expand your concentration when reading textbook materials. It makes use of the road signs provided by text authors and permits you to navigate a text chapter and prepare it for study.

1. **Survey it: Seeing the whole thing.** Textbook chapters vary in length from about twenty pages to sometimes more than seventy-five pages. But as a general rule of thumb, most college textbooks have chapters that are roughly twenty-five pages long. If you begin reading this word package with anticipatory knowledge of its length and basic content, you will understand what you read better and remember it longer. Do two survey things:

   First, write on the title page of the chapter the starting and ending page numbers for the chapter (for example, 135–160). Draw a box around the numbers if you like, or simply use parentheses. These numbers tell you the length of your journey for the first reading and all subsequent study sessions. In effect, every time you open to this chapter, you will know how far you must travel, and at various points in the study or reading session you will know how far you have come. Thus in this example, when you are on page 147, you know you've traveled half way. Or when you're on page 155, you can console yourself that you have only five pages to go, and so on.

   Second, before actually reading the chapter for the first time:

   - Leaf through all of its pages.

   - Scan the headings.

   - Read a sentence or two that starts the first paragraph after each heading.

   - Read completely the chapter summary at the end of the chapter.

   - For now, ignore illustrations or charts.

   - Devote no more than five to seven minutes to survey activities for a 25-page chapter. Longer than this, and you defeat the purpose.

This procedure is a real "survey" that permits you to get a grasp of the whole chapter before tackling each of its discrete parts. In your head, you will have a basic plan of the chapter as the author envisioned it. Some texts also provide a brief overview of the chapter at the start (e.g., *Merlin's* "About This Chapter" sections). Read this prefatory section as well, but focus on the chapter summary because it contains a real road map of the whole.

2. **Read it: With a pencil in your hand.** Never read anything without a pencil or dark-ink pen in your hand. Despite the marketing blitz and their widespread use, highlighting pens work against you in marking a text. A highlighter lays down translucent colored ink that draws your attention to the words you've marked. But highlighting does not make the *words* stand out; it merely draws your attention to a particular location on the page, and the words do not enter visual or semantic memory efficiently. The reason is a well-studied perceptual effect known as the Von Restorff phenomenon that Gestalt psychologists studied in the 1930s and '40s. The practical point here is that highlighting words will draw your attention to them, but it diminishes the meaning of the words and your capacity to visualize them.

A better way is to make the words, not their location, stand out in your visual and semantic memory. Dark-colored pencils or pens used to underline and mark important passages as you read are the best bet. They're cheap, simple, and perceptually efficient. Most books are printed with dark black ink, and underlining with pencil forces the eye to the words and their meanings without obscuring everything in the forest of words.

Create a system whereby you underline important ideas as you read and make a marginal notation with arrows to ideas you regard as worth remembering later when you study this chapter. Use abbreviations to mark passages that you want to reread without reading the whole page again. For example, a capital Q alongside a quoted passage in a text tells you at a glance to reread those memorable words when studying but to ignore the surrounding words because you already know the context for the quote from previous readings. Arrows or vertical straight lines are similarly effective.

Your goal when reading like this is to reduce each page of text to the important minimums that you will study and memorize for tests. A textbook page of 300 to 500 words can be read and reduced to sometimes fewer than 75 words. Some students underline or notate nearly everything but the pictures on a page. If you find yourself doing this, you might as well simply draw a circle around the whole thing.

Here are some tips for how to detect the most important things on a textbook page that deserve your attention and your pencil:

- The first sentence after a major heading usually states the central idea for a whole chapter section or subsection. That's why it's first.

- Headings, in general, follow a pattern within a text. Usually there are three levels, distinguished by their type size or style. For example, here are three head levels:

Main Heading to Begin Large Section

Second-Level Head for a Few Key Concepts

Third-Level Head for One or Two Specifics

Note, too, that the main head above is centered, whereas some subheads are placed at the left margin and some are indented slightly. Sometimes placement is the clue.

Always, consistency is maintained from chapter to chapter. The bigger the head, the higher the level of organization, with the smallest heads representing more precise details about a topic than the bigger (upper-level) heads. Look again through *Merlin* and you'll see that three different head levels are used throughout, with not only type size but graphic enhancements such as boxes to guide you.

- Contemporary texts use *italic type* and **boldface type** to emphasize ideas and to indicate important terms. These typographical conventions help alert you to terms you need to know, but they are no substitute for your own underlining and writing in margins.

It should be no surprise to you that reading this way takes time. Expect to spend two to three hours reading a text chapter this way. It is time well spent, because when you are ready to study the material for tests, you will be able to do three or four such chapters in the same time. And you will be prepared to understand, absorb, and make use of the material.

3. **Recite it : Rehearse what you remember.** When you have read your text chapter with a pencil in your hand, you should spend some time after each major section saying out loud to yourself the main ideas you can recall from that section. Merlin recommends pacing up and down your room with the book in your hand as you do this recital. It's not that pacing is more effective, but it is more dramatic and the great intellectual effort you're expending impresses others.

Your "recital" should be cumulative. As you finish each major section of the chapter and recite aloud what you recall, you should add to the recital the ideas you can recall from the previous sections.

By the end of the last section, therefore, your out-loud rehearsal includes a grocery list of all the key ideas you have grasped from the total chapter—in one gulp. While studying this material at a later date for a test, jot down the ideas as you study them again—a kind of written rehearsal for the upcoming test.

4. **Review it: Make it stick.** After rehearsal, close the book. In your mind's eye (or aloud, for that matter), review the whole chapter coherently rather than as a list of ideas. That is to say, tell yourself the "story" of the chapter. Struggle with the sequence of ideas as presented in what you read. Try to make one idea flow logically from the previous ones.

In effect, try to detect the main theme or themes that your text author was communicating. You'll be surprised how sensible it all seems when you do this, and how much you recall. Most important, with the book closed, you have to rely on your own logic and memory to fill in gaps, smooth rough spots, and make concepts follow sequentially.

Merlin suggests imagining yourself to be a teacher of the material. Instruct an imaginary audience in the main ideas. Not only will you remember them better this way, but you are preparing yourself for the last component of the Survey 3RQ method.

5. **Question it: Take the test before the test.** By the time you have surveyed, read, recited, and reviewed, you should really know the material in that chapter. Probably you know it as well as the teacher who assigned it. Make up questions you would ask about that material on a test if you wanted to make sure your students had learned it.

   Questions rarely are tricks, as discussed in Chapter 5. And most teachers construct questions that reflect the main points in the readings they have assigned. Be slightly more nitpicking than this, and you will in effect anticipate the test before you take it.

   In my experience, students who create and ask themselves questions about reading material almost always anticipate more than 90 percent of what I will put on the test. And even when their questions don't exactly match mine, their preparation in this way is more than sufficient for them to answer my questions completely and well.

   If you want to test this statement, try the method and write down your questions before each exam during your study period. Then keep track of how many times you score a hit. If your average is lower than nine out of ten times right, Merlin will turn your old car into a new BMW.

Two Ideas for Good Study

The point of the Survey 3RQ method is to prepare text material and yourself for more efficient study. But eventually, you have to study the material. Even reading with this active approach is not sufficient to master or retain the material. Here are two additional pieces of information drawn from psychological research that may help you when you get down to studying.

HOW TO READ A TEXTBOOK, AND WHY

A good deal of evidence from verbal-learning studies shows that the average person has better recall for memorized material about twenty-four hours after memorizing than immediately after memorizing it. The effect is called "reminiscence," and one hypothesis states that it results from an active neurological process whereby brain cells consolidate information while they are at rest.

Individuals differ, of course, but, in general, a practical technique can be derived from this research. When you have to study for an important test, plan your study so that you get some sleep (a good eight to nine hours) before the test. And do not restudy or do last-minute cramming as you go into a test. For reminiscence to work in your favor, you must not interfere with what you memorized by attempting to add more information or even reviewing well-learned information right before you get to recall what you've learned well.

The key point, of course, is that you learned the material well in the first place. Otherwise, your hungry neurons have nothing to consolidate. The best way to permit consolidation to occur is to go to sleep shortly after a study session. No television, no books, magazines, or trips to the pub. Just sleep.

No one said college was easy.

The second technique involves the terrible circumstance of having to study for two tests to be taken the same day. Research on retroactive and proactive inhibition has shown that the more similar two kinds of verbal material are, the more they interfere with each other during learning and during recall.

BALBOA DARWIN, BELOVED COUSIN OF CHARLES.

The practical lesson for test taking, then, is that if you must study two similar subjects, time your study sessions so that they are not both done the same day. Thus, for example, studying for an English literature test and a mathematics test will interfere with each other less than studying for a biology test and a psychology test on the same day.

Sometimes, as during final exams, cramming for two tests is unavoidable. Do the wisest thing: Separate your studying of similar subjects by at least a day and do not review one subject right after studying another.

And sleep.

Taking Lecture Notes the Merlin Way

The key ingredient in the Survey 3RQ method is being active rather than passive with text materials. Exactly the same strategy is useful for taking notes in class.

Some students approach a lecture class with a kind of passivity more appropriate to watching a stage performance or a television program. Sitting and watching a lecturer, taking down an occasional note or two, is a waste of your time.

Other students feel apprehensive and attempt to record every word the prof utters. Even if you take shorthand, a two-hour class of verbatim notetaking will drain you to the point of not ever wanting to hear that prof's voice again. Tape-recording a class is not much help for the same reason. If you tape a two-hour class, it takes two hours to listen to the class—again.

If you approach a lecture class with an active processing strategy to notetaking, you will reduce a two-hour class to a few pages of workable notes. In addition, you open yourself to the thinking skills of the teacher, all those cognitive strategies a skilled prof can model. Like the Survey 3RQ method, which prepares text materials into a personal, edited format briefer than the original, a good notetaking style transforms class presentations into your personalized briefer format. That's why they're called "*note*books" and not books. Here are some Merlin hints about efficient notetaking:

- Listen actively without trying to record the exact words of the lecturer. Get the ideas contained in his or her sentences, and write them down in brief phrases. Out of every three or four sentences uttered by a speaker, only one or a half of one sentence is worth recording. The rest is verbiage designed to illustrate or amplify. If you're listening, you will be able to amplify later when you read your notes.

- Every good lecturer tells you what the main ideas are, and frequently to emphasize the point, writes them on the chalkboard. Follow these clues and use the written notations as headings or main breaks in your notes.

- When a lecturer uses a diagram or a chart, start a separate page in your notebook automatically. Feel free to turn the pages sideways for column tables or charts, and to draw or scribble diagrams as appropriate.

- Rewriting your notes to make them neater is not especially useful. If you do it correctly in class, you will save enormous time and relieve yourself of the burden of redoing notes endlessly. It's like taking notes on a textbook chapter. If you underline and read it Survey 3RQ style, you don't need the notes. It's done. Efficiently. Regard lecture notes the same way. You are already spending your time in the class taking the notes and assimilating the information. Don't beat it to death.

- If you miss a class, borrow someone's notes to get the information. But, as we all know, someone else's notes are never as good as your own, because they do not trigger the memories of the actual class which permit you to fill in the gaps and organize the material in your head. Think of borrowed notes as a last resort—better than nothing.

- Finally, as discussed in Chapter 5, when it comes time to study for tests, it is usually better to begin with lecture notes from the class and then proceed to the text and other readings. Lectures are really a road map of those concepts regarded as most important by the prof. Your notes are also an exquisitely precise guide to what you should emphasize from the readings and how to organize the wealth of information.

 M

Dear Activist,

After you graduate, photocopy your old notebooks from the really inept professors, and mail copies to them. This way, they can see what they have taught you. Think of this activity as "sharing" your experiences, and as giving feedback to your teachers. Or, if you prefer, focus on the sleepless nights you will cause incompetent twits when they try to figure out why all these copies of handwritten, disorganized, ludicrous class notes keep showing up in their mailboxes. Remember: *after* you graduate.

Love,

Merlin

Writing Papers the Merlin Way

A survival guide would not be complete without some sorcery for paper writing. *Merlin* is not the place to detail how-to skills, which are better taught in the context of a particular discipline. Every major academic discipline has its own format, or style sheet. Matters of style, such as footnotes and citations of references, are in one format for departments of English or philosophy and in another for the social and natural sciences. Your major discipline will no doubt introduce you to the style manual that it requires.

You should also be aware that writing is a learnable skill, and most colleges have programs that directly teach these skills or that teach methods for improving basic skills. The best way to learn to write well is to read good writing. The second best way is to write under apprenticeship to a good writer who is also a good editor and who can give you necessary feedback to help you acquire an ear and an eye for good writing.

What *Merlin* can address are some important issues about the process of producing papers, with a focus on dispelling some myths that surround papers and some blunt advice about profiting educationally from the papers you write. Problems with procrastination and plagiarism are also fair game.

Profiting from Your Papers

Profs assign term papers because they want to teach you something about the area of knowledge the paper focuses on. Most traditional term papers involve research in the library to survey what others have written. The theory is that by compelling you to read a large amount of writing on a single topic, organize it, synthesize it, and report it with appropriate quotations and references, you will become familiar with those ideas.

That theory worked in medieval universities, and sometimes works at the graduate or professional level of education. The reason: Graduate and professional students are held accountable for what they learn in this way. Eventually they have to demonstrate that the knowledge they got from writing term papers is really in their heads. Usually this demonstration takes the form of comprehensive exams, or dissertation research, or state licensing exams to enter a profession.

Most of the time, term papers at the undergraduate level do not accomplish much in the way of learning. Students find them burdensome and boring to write. Professors find them burdensome and boring to read. Students find ways to hand in papers they have not researched, have not written, or have not even seen before. It is a terrible game.

I have known students who bought a term paper from suppliers who stock virtually any topic you can name, in any grade quality for which you are willing to pay. Sometimes these students get caught; most of the time they do not. All of the time, *they* are cheated by this practice.

Here is the only good reason I can think of for writing term papers: You will expose yourself to two intellectual processes modeled by the people whose work you read and borrow to report with, one hopes, appropriate reference citations.

First, you will learn about the process of inquiry by which stored information can be retrieved through reading books, journals, or printouts at a computer terminal. You will learn firsthand that if you have a question, somewhere in the world of ideas you can find an answer or an approach to an answer. Most important, you will learn how to devise appropriate questions that can be answered. This skill is so important that it is worth the whole price of a college education.

Second, you will learn to synthesize, or integrate, or harmonize discrete bits of information into whole concepts. By struggling with the conflicting, differing, sometimes complementary ideas of people focused on a single topic, you will learn how to make information sensible, how to tease ideas from mere data, how to make intellectual reality sensible. You will be critical rather than naive, informed rather than ignorant, and alert to contradictions rather than apathetic.

The price you pay for acquiring these skills is writing term papers, probably on topics that have been written about ad nauseam since the first student applied to the first teacher for lessons. (Her name, by the

way, was Arabella, and her assigned
topic was "Gender differences in rearing
the cave-dwelling child." It's a fact. You
could look it up.)

Some thinking teachers have begun
to look for alternate ways to help students learn these same skills without the
traditional term paper song and dance of organized plagiarism with
references. Term projects requiring students to apply what they learn
in a course to real cases or real problems have become more widespread. Psychology students research a real clinical case of one
patient, business students research one case study of a business
enterprise, and mathematics students research one real computer
problem for which no answer yet exists. And the list is growing.

If you want to take from college something of value, don't buy your
papers, don't borrow them, and don't toss them off. Write them, and
ask your teachers how to write them well. The act of knowing which
expert to ask for help is part of the process of inquiry.

Procrastination

Procrastination is a topic that ought to be saved for last, but Merlin
hates tradition. Psychologist Philip Cristantiello described the procras-
tinator this way:

> Procrastinators have a strained relationship with time and tasks.
> They are nearly always wanting—and waiting—for conditions to be
> a little better. The book of Ecclesiastes tells us that "To everything
> there is a season." Yet to the procrastinator carrying on a love
> affair with eternity, things are always out of season.

Writing papers is the single college experience that yields to procrastination better than anything short of filing income taxes. Papers
frequently are completed the night before they are due, and they show
it. The student who does this also shows it—in wear and tear, bleary
eyes, and an increased reluctance to do the next paper.

The reasons for procrastination are almost as varied as term paper topics, but they share a common underlying belief: Putting off the task saves us from confronting the possibility of criticism, of not doing well, of not being as adequate as we would like to believe. Here are some correctives:

- Believe that things don't happen until they do.

- Know that there is no more time than there is.

- Understand that intelligence is not related to perfection.

- Realize that personal limits don't excuse meeting realistic goals.

- Tell yourself the truth: Writing papers is hard. It's supposed to be.

Plagiarism

Don't. Ever.

Deliberate plagiarism is stealing and lying combined. Everyone knows it is wrong. It cheats the student of his or her education, it robs the person whose words or ideas are taken, and it deceives the teacher who assigned work in good faith. What more need be said?

Plenty. In my experience, a great deal of plagiarism is not deliberate. It results from ineptitude, lack of writing skills, and fear of not doing well. Students have a difficult time distinguishing between paraphrasing published ideas and quoting them with reference citations. Here are some guidelines to help you distinguish between when it is acceptable to paraphrase without citing your sources and when it is not.

- Taking the exact words of another, no matter how brief the excerpt, requires quotation marks and a footnote or citation of the author's name and date of publication. Exact words require acknowledgment.

- Exact ideas expressed in your own words but originating in the writing of another person require citation of the source. Period. If it's someone else's idea, give him or her credit.

- Ideas, phrases, or combinations of ideas partially expressed as in the original source but partly changed require citation of the source and may require some explanation of what kind of changes you have introduced.

- It is always permissible to write about another's ideas; it is always permissible to use another's ideas; it is always permissible to quote another's words, or reproduce another's images. Fair sharing of ideas is what the life of the mind is about. All that is required is giving credit. For publishing purposes, obtaining permission from the published source of the quotation is always prudent. But this is a detail you will rarely need to consider at the college level.

- When in doubt about whether to cite a reference or not, especially when it's been cited already in your paper, cite it again anyway. Always err on the side of giving too much credit.

- Unless an idea has been so elegantly, so beautifully, or so skillfully expressed that rephrasing it would destroy the idea, paraphrase it with your own words and give credit to the original. In this way you begin to assimilate the great ideas of others and build your stock of personal familiarity with literature, art, philosophy—in short, familiarity with the world of the intellect.

It is a truism of almost absolute magnitude that writing a term paper by definition excludes original ideas. Your job, remember, is usually to survey the published literature in a particular area. You may create thereby a unique synthesis or a unique perspective on that group of writings, but to do so you have to report the ideas of others.

No one expects a term paper to be original thinking in the strictest sense of that term. But everyone expects the paper to be original *with you.* Borrow ideas, and borrow them wisely. But don't appear to claim them as your own by failing to acknowledge the original writers. There is no shame to a term paper overly footnoted. There is a great deal to one without sufficient citations.

Some Summary, Some Conclusions

☆ Merlin's secret of the universe: Words and pictures are the languages of ideas, and most often you will find them in textbooks.

☆ A textbook author shares ideas with you, so that acquiring ideas from a text is really a sharing of minds.

☆ Reading a text requires a kind of attention different from that required when reading a novel or short story. You must provide the cohesion and links between ideas, and you must provide the sustained effort to make it memorable.

☆ The Merlin adaptation of a well-known reading method, Survey 3RQ, calls for active participation with the author by doing these things:

1. *Survey* the whole chapter, with attention to headings and subheadings.

2. *Read* the chapter with a pencil in your hand to underline and make notes.

3. *Recite* what you recall after each section aloud as rehearsal.

4. *Review* what you've read at the end of the chapter by creating a cohesive "story" of the main chapter themes.

5. *Question* yourself by creating the questions you would ask if you were teaching this material.

☆ Writing papers and taking notes are extensions of the Survey 3RQ method: the key is to be active, attentive, and timely. Plagiarism and procrastination are major obstacles to learning from the experience of paper writing.

Where Merlin's Ideas
Come From:
Further Readings

Chapter 1: Student Survival Styles

Throughout the history of psychology, theorists have described a vast number of personality styles in their theories of human nature. Key thinkers who influenced the presentation of the student styles of Darwin, Damocles, and Merlin are (in order of importance):

Horney, Karen. *Neurosis and Human Growth.* New York: Norton, 1950.

Fromm, Erich. *To Have or to Be?* New York: Harper & Row, 1976.

Atkinson, J. W. *An Introduction to Motivation* (1st ed.) (especially his chapters on his own conception of the fear of failure and need-achieving personalities). New York: Van Nostrand, 1964. Atkinson has published several presentations of his work more recently, but they tend to be mathematical presentations. This textbook account remains the classic statement. See also Atkinson, J. W., and Birch, D., *Introduction to Motivation* (2nd ed.). New York: Van Nostrand, 1978.

Allport, Gordon. *Becoming: Basic Considerations for a Psychology of Personality.* New Haven: Yale University Press, 1955.

Maslow, Abraham. *Motivation and Personality* (2nd ed.). New York: Harper & Row, 1970.

Chapter 2: The Care and Feeding of Professors

The thinkers listed for Chapter 1 could appropriately be acknowledged for this chapter as well. In addition, the following thinkers influenced the presentation of professor types and ways to deal with them (in order of importance):

Shapiro, David. *Neurotic Styles.* New York: Harper & Row (Basic Books), 1965.

Kohut, Heinz. *The Restoration of the Self.* New York: International Universities Press, 1975.

Freud, Sigmund. "Repression." 1915. In Vol. XIV of *The Standard Edition of the Complete Psychological Works of Sigmund Freud.* Edited by James Strachey. London: Hogarth Press, 1957.

Kelly, George A. "A Psychology of the Optimal Man." In *Personal Construct Psychology,* edited by A. W. Landfield and L. M. Leitner. New York: Wiley, 1980.

Chapter 3: So You Have to Major in Something

Roe, Anne, and Sigelman, R. *The Origin of Interests.* Washington, D.C.: APGA Inquiry Studies, No. 1, 1964.

Roe, Anne. *The Making of a Scientist.* New York: Dodd, Mead, 1953.

White, Robert. *The Enterprise of Living* (2nd ed.). New York: Holt, Rinehart & Winston, 1976. See especially chapters 16 to 20.

Rogers, Carl. *On Becoming a Person.* Boston: Houghton Mifflin, 1961.

Chapter 4: Getting Them to Teach and Advise You

In order of importance:

The concept of *schmooze* along with a host of other wonderful words can be found in Leo Rosten's dictionary *The Joys of Yiddish*. New York: Washington Square Paperback, 1968.

Rogers, Carl. "The Necessary and Sufficient Conditions of Therapeutic Personality Change." *Journal of Consulting Psychology*, 21 (1957) 95–103.

Chapter 5: How to Take Tests

In order of importance:

Spielberger, Charles, and Sarason, Irwin, eds. *Stress and Anxiety*. Vol. 5. New York: Wiley, 1978. See especially chapters 1, 9, 10, 11—each by a different author.

Sieber, J. E., O'Neil, H. F. Jr., and Tobias, S. *Anxiety, Learning, and Instruction*. New York: Lawrence Erlbaum Associates, 1977.

Yerkes, R. M., and Dodson, J. D. "The Relationship of Strength of Stimulas to Rapidity of Habit Formation." *Journal of Comparative and Physiological Psychology* 18 (1980): 459–82.

Zeigarnik, Bluma. "On Finished and Unfinished Tasks." 1927. In *A Source Book of Gestalt Psychology*, edited by Willis D. Ellis. New York: Humanities Press, 1967.

Solso, Robert. *Cognitive Psychology*. New York: Harcourt Brace Jovanovich, 1979. See especially the chapters that review the fine work on memory, verbal learning, and cognitive organization.

Chapter 6: How to Read a Textbook, and Why

In order of importance:

Robinson, F. P. *Effective Study*. New York: Harper & Row, 1961.

Thomas, E. L., and Robinson, H. A. *Improving Reading in Every Class: A Sourcebook for Teachers*. Boston: Allyn & Bacon, 1972.

Cristantiello, Philip. "Procrastination." *Review for Religious*. Sept.-Oct. 1987, 720–25.

Tolman, E. C. "Cognitive Maps in Mice and Men." *Psychological Review* 55 (1948): 189–208.

Apple Computer Co. Developers Association. *Human Interface Guidelines*. Cupertino, Calif.: Apple Computer Inc., 1986. See especially chapters 1 and 2 on rationale and philosophy.

Lewin, Kurt. *Principles of Topological Psychology*. New York: McGraw-Hill, 1936. See especially the sections on Aristotelian versus Galilean thinking.

Roszak, Theodore. *The Cult of Information*. New York: Pantheon (Random House), 1986. See chapter 5 on master ideas and chapter 10 on thinking.

Tell Merlin . . .

If you have some thoughts about *Merlin*, share them by writing your ideas in the spaces below and returning this page to *Merlin*.

c/o: Dr. Christopher F. Monte
Manhattanville College
Purchase, New York 10577

Thank you.

What I found most helpful about *Merlin* was:

What I found least helpful about *Merlin* was:

About myself (name is optional):